THE GREAT BRITISH
BAKE OFF

The Big Book of
AMAZING CAKES

THE GREAT BRITISH
BAKE OFF

The Big Book of
AMAZING CAKES

sphere

CONTENTS

FOREWORD

A NOTE FROM PAUL

I can't believe it's been ten years! I've been so lucky to have been a part of *The Great British Bake Off* with Sandi, Noel and Prue. We are constantly amazed and inspired by what the bakers come up with – every year brings new surprises – and the cakes made on the show always influence the baking community in a massive way.

This book is a celebration of cakes – some of the best bakers' recipes and technicals from this and past series, along with many more recipes for all levels of bakers. We want this to be the ultimate book for all cake bakers, with beautiful, delicious and achievable cakes for everyone to make, reflecting the best of *Bake Off* cake-making.

Prue and I love coming up with the challenges – and the recipes in this book bring back so many memories from the series and the challenges we have set. Have a go at making the cakes in the comfort of your own home and become a star baker – and maybe even a winner – in your own kitchen.

A NOTE FROM PRUE

The first cake I ever baked was a Christmas cake at school. It took the whole term's lessons to make. It was iced with royal icing and I was immeasurably proud of it. But I hadn't put any glycerine into the icing and it set like concrete. My father broke my mother's favourite knife trying to cut it.

Not a good start. But since then I've baked hundreds of cakes; more so since being part of this show. *Bake Off* has been truly inspiring. Every week on this series we saw something completely different, wildly imaginative or just utterly delicious.

It's a real pleasure to see such an extensive collection of cakes in this book, from the classics to the grand occasion cakes. Even the most complicated of them have step-by-step instructions so that anyone should be able to pick up the book and bake a great cake. We have recipes from the series and family favourites from this year's bakers, as well as irresistible recipes old and new that just can't be left out of a cake book.

I hope and trust, and indeed believe, that these recipes will have you reaching for a mixing bowl. And once started, you will keep going.

INTRODUCTION

This book provides the definitive celebration of cake. Featuring amazing cakes in all their guises (from well-loved classics to vegan bakes and from cupcakes to fondant fancies), we have brought together the ultimate *The Great British Bake Off* collection, aiming to excite and inspire, as well as – of course – to introduce you to our Series 10 bakers. As *Bake Off* celebrates its tenth birthday, we've also included a selection of the amazing cakes from the previous series, and you'll also find plenty of new cake recipes to get stuck into.

Chapters on classic, chocolate, fruit & nut and free-from cakes each open with a perfect example of a cake in that category (the Victoria Sponge in Classics, the Ultimate Chocolate Cake in Chocolate, the Traditional Fruit Cake in Fruit & Nut, and the Vegan Lemon Drizzle in Free-from). Each of these recipes is followed by a table that gives you recipe quantities for alternative sizes and shapes of that cake, so that you can adapt and experiment to create something that's just right for you. Then, every chapter features page after delicious page of other cake delights, each presented with clear, step-by-step instructions that leave nothing to chance.

A further chapter, sitting at the very heart of the book, is a personal glimpse into the worlds of the Series 10 bakers, featuring their own family favourites and including some of the cakes that inspired them to start baking themselves.

Icons at the top of each recipe show how many people each cake serves, and hands-on times to give you a sense of how long you can expect to spend gathering your ingredients, and then mixing, and decorating your cake. The baking time is an instant guide to how long the baked elements of each cake will need in the oven (always follow the precise baking times given in the method).

Before you get started, read our guide to the chemistry of baking, which includes information on the role of each key ingredient, and how to use your oven to get the best results, every time. And, because we want to inspire you not only to create the amazing cakes in the book, but also invent your own, information on the key methods of making cakes will help you to grow in confidence and experiment in your own kitchen. The storage information on page 20 will help you to keep your cake for longer should you have any left over, or if you are saving your bake for a particular day. Finally, throughout the book, key techniques (piping cupcakes, decorating with chocolate and creating a showstopping naked effect) provide you with simple, step-by-step guidance on how to make the very most of your own amazing cakes.

On your marks, get set, bake!

THE CHEMISTRY OF CAKE-MAKING

Cake-making requires precision and a fundamental respect for the science that goes into every recipe. This might sound daunting, but actually it's the opposite: as long as you weigh your ingredients precisely and follow the method carefully, you should get the right result every time. Here are a few Bake Off insights into the chemistry within every cake.

THE INGREDIENTS

At its simplest a cake is a combination of flour, eggs, sugar, fat (in the form of butter, spread or oil) and perhaps a raising agent (such as baking powder or bicarbonate of soda). It's a short list, but each ingredient does a specific job in the chemistry of cake-making, and the combination of ingredients gives you the taste, texture and rise you want. That's why accurate weighing and measuring are so important.

Flour
Flour gives your cake structure. Wheat flour contains protein in varying amounts, which when mixed with liquid forms gluten. Stretchy and elastic, gluten provides the strength that holds a cake together. But you want exactly the right amount of gluten – too much and a cake will be tough; too little and it will be too tender. Most recipes stipulate to fold the flour gently into the creamed or whisked cake batter – this is to avoid over-developing the gluten in the flour.

From nuts and pulses to grains, flour can be made from many different core ingredients, but most traditional cakes require wheat-based plain white flour (which usually calls for the addition of a raising agent, such as baking powder) or self-raising flour (which already has raising agents in it). Sifting the flour is particularly important when making cakes, as it gets rid of any lumps and adds air.

Gluten-free baking
Gluten-free flour is made from rice, nuts, buckwheat, potatoes, chestnuts, oats or chickpeas – or a combination of them. These flours don't naturally produce gluten, so gluten-free recipes usually use either xanthan gum or guar gum to help produce a cake-like texture, keeping the cake moist and stopping it falling apart. Gluten-free flours labelled specifically for cake baking have gum already incorporated, but if you are making your own gluten-free mixture, add in the gum with the dry ingredients, as it is more difficult to combine once you have added the liquid. Making gluten-free cakes is not as straightforward as substituting wheat flour for gluten-free – the amount of liquid, the baking time and the baking temperature may also change. As always, then, follow the recipe.

Sugar

Sugar gives a cake much more than just sweetness. It keeps a cake moist and, after baking, gives it its wonderful golden colour. Like all the other ingredients, it also has a critical role to play in the production of air. Sugar both helps to create air bubbles during the creaming or whisking stage and interferes with the development of gluten in the flour, guaranteeing the finished cake a light, tender texture.

Different types of sugar and sweeteners have different effects on a cake. Most recipes will call for caster sugar, especially if the cake uses the creaming method (see page 17), as the small crystals of caster sugar enable more bubbles to form, increasing the lightness of a cake. Dark brown sugar will produce a richer colour and flavour, but also a denser texture. Honey, molasses, golden syrup and treacle – which caramelise as they cook – are often used in cakes made with the melting method (see page 19) and result in a dense, moist cake with less air, such as gingerbread.

Eggs

When you beat eggs together with fat and sugar, they create a light foam – bubbles of air attach themselves to the uneven edges of the sugar crystals and the layer of fat holds them in place. When cakes heat up in the oven, the air in the foam expands and the eggs solidify around the bubbles to keep them intact. This creates the final structure of the cake. Eggs also help to create that beautiful golden-brown colour of cakes.

Most recipes call for eggs at room temperature and to add them gradually to avoid the mixture curdling (although adding a little flour will fix the problem; see page 17).

Fat

In the form of butter, spread or oil, fat keeps cakes moist and adds flavour. But perhaps fat's most important job is to coat the flour molecules, protecting them from the egg or milk, which would cause more gluten to form and produce a heavier cake. Fat also traps air, creating lots of tiny air bubbles.

Preferences vary when it comes to which fat to use – some bakers argue that butter tastes better, while others say spreads are best for creaming, as they tend to be softer and are better at trapping air during mixing. Either way, the fat needs to be at room temperature before use, because if it is too cold, it won't absorb much air. Cakes, such as carrot cake, made using the melting method (see page 19), which have a moist texture and dense crumb, often call for vegetable oils.

Raising agents

Also known as chemical leavening agents, raising agents, as their name suggests, help a cake to rise. The most common are baking powder and bicarbonate of soda. These react with moisture in the cake mixture to create carbon dioxide gas, which fills and expands the air bubbles that were created during creaming or whisking. Always measure the amount of raising agent carefully, as too much can taint the flavour of a cake; and always mix bicarbonate of soda with an acid ingredient, such as yogurt, buttermilk or cream of tartar, to activate it.

THE BAKING

It's not just the ingredients that require careful attention in baking cakes. The method and the equipment you use (and how you use it) are just as important, so here are a few general tips to help you. As always, follow the recipe carefully and all should be fine.

Baking tins

Size matters when it comes to baking tins, so always use the size, shape and depth specified in the recipe. (Changing the size or shape of the tin will affect the baking time.)

Any style of tin is obviously going to do the job, but if you have a choice, a dull, light-coloured tin is preferable to a shiny one (which will reflect heat) or a dark one (which will absorb too much heat and might over-bake your cake). Generally, a good-quality, durable tin will distribute the heat evenly.

Preparing your tin properly is also key. Do this before you start making your mixture, so that the tin is ready to use as soon as the mixture is ready.

Ovens

Get to know your oven because ovens vary in accuracy. If you can, use an oven thermometer and be aware that fan-assisted convection ovens cook cakes faster than conventional ovens. All our recipes include the conventional and equivalent fan temperatures, but the rule of thumb is to reduce the non-fan baking temperature by about 20°C/68°F if you're using a fan oven.

Make sure you've heated the oven to the correct temperature before putting the cake inside. If you start baking the cake when the temperature is too low, your cake probably won't rise and may even have a sunken top.

If the oven is too high, your cake will cook too quickly on the outside, have a peaked top, and will probably burn.

In a conventional (non-fan) oven, the middle shelf of the oven is best for cake-baking, to avoid burning the top of the cake. However, if you have a convection fan-assisted oven, where you position the cake shouldn't be an issue, as the fan will evenly distribute the heat. Never slam the door of your oven with the cake inside, as the vibration can burst the air bubbles in the sponge, causing the cake to sink – and try not to open the door at all during baking, as the resulting change in temperature can also make the cake sink.

'Doneness'

So, after all that, how do you know when your cake is ready to come out of the oven? As ovens can vary, this is a bit less scientific. Check the cake 5–10 minutes either side of the given baking time. Start by turning the light on in the oven, rather than opening the door, unless you really think your cake is ready. If your cake is looking brown on top and starting to shrink slightly from the edge of the tin, open the oven. A cake that's done should produce a lovely, biscuity smell. If it's a whisked cake, touch the top gently with your finger – it should spring back; if it's a creamed cake, insert a skewer into the middle – it should come out clean. (If there's cake mixture on the skewer, you need to bake the cake for a little longer and test again.)

Cooling

When you take the cake out of the oven, most recipes suggest giving it 5–10 minutes to cool in the tin before releasing and cooling it on a wire rack. Unless specified otherwise, if you leave the cake in the tin, it will continue to bake and may overcook.

METHODS OF MAKING CAKES

Watch a series of Bake Off and you'll learn pretty quickly that there are a few subtly different ways to make a cake. It's all about how you combine the various ingredients, and whether you mix the butter and sugar first, or just add everything at once.

CREAMING METHOD

For a creamed cake, mix the softened butter (or the spread) with the sugar before adding the dry ingredients. Beat until the mixture becomes pale in colour and has a light, creamy consistency. Some recipes suggest beating the butter (or spread) first on its own until pale and creamy, then adding the sugar gradually while continuing to beat. You can beat the butter and sugar with a wooden spoon, or use an electric hand whisk or a stand mixer, usually on a medium speed. The length of time you'll need to beat obviously depends on the method you use, but it can range from 3-20 minutes for creaming by hand with a wooden spoon. This method adds lots of air to the mixture, which helps the cake to rise and gives it a light texture.

After creaming together the butter and sugar, beat the eggs in one at a time (or if the ingredients calls for beaten eggs, add them little by little) to prevent the cake batter curdling. The protein in the eggs stretches with the continued beating, holding the tiny air bubbles in place. Finally, fold in the flour gently to ensure you keep as much air as possible in the mixture.

This method is used to make cakes such as the classic Victoria Sponge (see page 25) and the Blackberry Pound Cake (see page 182).

Creaming tips

» Make sure the butter or spread is at room temperature for easy creaming. People often pop it in the microwave to soften it – but be careful: if it's too soft, or melting, the cake will not rise well.

» Caster sugar is the best sugar to use for a creamed cake as it has small grains, unlike granulated sugar, and gives a pale and fluffy texture. Larger grains may result in a speckled appearance and crunchy texture after baking; while icing sugar is too fine and powdery.

» If the cake mixture curdles when you add the eggs, add a tablespoonful of the flour (or flour mixture) with each addition of egg to help stabilise it. When the batter is smooth, fold in the remaining flour.

» When folding in the flour, use a large metal spoon and a gentle figure of eight movement until mixed in – this will keep in as much air as possible.

WHISKING METHOD

This method is usually used for lower-fat, lighter sponges, such as a roulades or Swiss rolls. Whisking the eggs and sugar replaces the need for a raising agent, such as baking powder or self-raising flour, to give the cake a light texture and good rise. Traditionally, you whisk the eggs and sugar together in a bowl set over a pan of gently simmering water until the mixture increases in volume by about four times and is thick enough to leave a ribbon trail when you lift the whisk. The mixture will also become pale and creamy.

Then, you fold in the flour in batches, taking care not to knock the air out of the mixture. Sometimes, such as with a génoise sponge, you add melted butter, which makes a light cake with a soft sponge. Angel cake (see page 63), on the other hand, is traditionally butter- and egg-yolk-free and is a delicate cake with a slightly dry texture.

Some recipes using the whisking method call for separating the eggs. In that case, you whisk the egg yolks with the sugar until pale, thick and creamy. Then, you whisk the egg whites separately until they reach stiff peaks, and then fold them in (alternately with the flour, if using). You'd use this method for a meringue cake, for example.

Whisking tips

» When whisking over a pan of water, do not allow the bowl to touch the water or the water to boil, as the mixture will become too hot and the eggs will start to scramble.

» Leave the cake batter to cool to room temperature before adding the flour.

» Bake the cake as soon as you've made it, as the whisked batter is unstable. It's particularly important with a whisked cake to avoid opening the oven until the cake is ready.

MELTING METHOD

This is perhaps one of the easiest methods for making cake as there's no beating or whisking involved to aerate the mixture. Instead, you melt the butter, usually with sugar, then add it to the eggs, followed by the dry ingredients, including plain flour with a raising agent, such as baking powder. This method produces a cake with a dense, moist crumb and is used for gingerbread and some brownies and blondies.

Melting tips

» Let the melted butter or butter–sugar mixture cool to room temperature before adding the eggs and dry ingredients.

» Fold the sifted dry ingredients into the wet ingredients, working as quickly as possible.

ALL-IN-ONE-CAKES

This method is exactly what it says it is, and couldn't be easier to make. You simply put all the ingredients in one bowl, mix them together with a wooden spoon or electric stand mixer and then bake in the oven. Vanilla, chocolate or coffee sponge cakes suit this method.

All-in-one tips

» When you sift in the dry ingredients, raise the sieve as high as you can above the bowl to maximise the flour's contact with the air.

» Try not to overmix the cake batter – you want to keep in every air bubble to make sure the cake rises properly.

HOW TO STORE A CAKE

WRAP IT UP

Cakes that are covered with icing tend to stay moist because the coating provides a natural wrapping that helps to retain the moisture in the cake. If your cake is topped with buttercream, store it in a cake tin or airtight plastic container lined with baking paper (in the fridge is best; see below). Note that strong flavours can taint a plastic container – a good wash to remove previous odours before using again is essential.

Undecorated sponges – whether whole or in slices – fare well wrapped in cling film. Wrap tightly with no gaps, to stop the cake from drying out. Cakes will store like this at cool room temperature for 1–2 weeks.

Fruit cakes encased in marzipan and icing will last much longer than regular sponges (up to a month, or even longer if laced with alcohol), but in this case use only a tin or a box for storage, as plastic can make the cake sweat and so go mouldy.

KEEP IT COOL

Cakes with buttercream or ganache topping will last for 3–4 days in the fridge, stored in an airtight container. If the cake has custard, cream, cream cheese or fresh fruit it will last 1–2 days at most. Allow any cake you have refrigerated to come up to room temperature before you serve it. Finally, avoid refrigerating cakes with sugar paste, fondant or food colouring, because the colours can bleed.

FREEZE IT

Undecorated sponges are perfect for freezing (freeze buttercream or icing separately, in an airtight container). Wrap the sponge well in cling film, add a layer of foil if you like, and then place in an airtight plastic container or re-sealable bag – this will stop your cake from absorbing other flavours in the freezer. You can freeze basic sponges for about 4 months.

Allow your cakes to defrost completely before serving (it can take about 3 hours for a Victoria sponge to defrost at room temperature). If you've frozen the buttercream, defrost it, add a splash of milk to loosen and whip it to make it fluffy and spreadable. If you need to level your sponges before decorating, defrost them first.

AND, FINALLY...

Even if you intend to eat your cake on the day, a few key tips will keep your cake at its best. Allow your cakes to cool completely on a wire rack before decorating – any residual steam or heat can cause icing to melt. While your cake is cooling and after decorating, keep the cake out of direct sunlight, which can dry out the sponge and discolour the icing.

If your kitchen is very warm, or if it's a hot summer's day, even if you plan to eat your cake within hours of baking, store it in the fridge until you're ready, leaving just enough time for it to come up to room temperature before serving.

CHAPTER ONE

Classics

This is the standard Victoria sponge recipe for two 20cm sponges to sandwich together, but it's easy to adapt for different shapes and sizes. Use the table on the following page to help you.

Victoria Sponge

FOR THE SPONGE
200g unsalted butter, softened
200g golden caster sugar
1 tsp vanilla paste
4 eggs, beaten
200g self-raising flour, sifted
1 tsp baking powder
150g homemade or good-
    quality strawberry jam
icing sugar, for dusting

FOR THE BUTTERCREAM
100g unsalted butter, softened
200g icing sugar, sifted
½ tsp vanilla paste

YOU WILL NEED
20cm sandwich tins x 2,
    greased, then base-lined
    with baking paper
large disposable piping bag
    (optional)

1 Heat the oven to 180°C/160°C fan/350°F/Gas 4 .

2 Beat the butter, sugar and vanilla in a stand mixer fitted with the beater, on medium speed for 5–6 minutes, until pale and creamy.

3 Add the eggs, a little at a time, beating well between each addition until well combined. If the mixture curdles, add 1 tablespoon of the flour and combine again.

4 In a separate bowl, use a fork to stir together the flour and baking powder. Then, fold the dry ingredients through the wet ingredients, until just incorporated.

5 Divide the cake mixture equally between the two sandwich tins. Bake for 25–30 minutes, until golden and springy and a skewer inserted into the centres comes out clean. Cool the sponges in the tins for 5 minutes, then turn out onto a wire rack to cool completely.

6 Make the buttercream. Beat the butter, icing sugar and vanilla together in a stand mixer fitted with the beater, on medium speed for 1–2 minutes, until fluffy.

7 To assemble, place one of the cooled sponges upside down on a cake plate or stand. Spread with jam, then spread the buttercream over the top. Alternatively, fill the piping bag with the buttercream and snip a 1cm hole in the end. Pipe the buttercream in little blobs around the outside edge of the sponge, then use a palette knife to swirl it in towards the centre to completely cover.

8 Place the second sponge on top. Press the sponges gently together, then dust with icing sugar before serving.

SCALING QUANTITIES
VICTORIA SPONGE

Use this table to adjust your Victoria sponge mixture according to the size or shape of cake you want to make. The quantities for the 25cm and 30cm round cakes are for two 5cm-deep cake tins. If you have only one tin, bake in two batches (half quantities for each batch), making one sponge, then repeating for a second.

	25cm round, deep tin	30cm round, deep tin	900g loaf tin	23 x 30cm traybake tin
For the sponge				
unsalted butter, softened	450g	700g	225g	250g
golden caster sugar	450g	700g	225g	250g
vanilla paste	3 tsp	2 tbsp	1 tsp	1 tsp
eggs, beaten	9	14	4	5
self-raising flour, sifted	450g	700g	250g	250g
baking powder	2 tsp	4 tsp	1 tsp	1 tsp
homemade/good-quality strawberry jam	300g	600g	3 tbsp	5 tbsp
For the buttercream				
unsalted butter, softened	150g	200g	75g	125g
icing sugar	300g	400g	150g	250g
vanilla paste	1½ tsp	2 tsp	½ tsp	1 tsp
Baking time @ 180°C/ 160°C fan/350°F/Gas 4	40–45 mins	45 mins	45–50 mins	25–30 mins

Named to honour the union of Queen Victoria's granddaughter with Prince Louis Battenberg in 1884, Battenberg sponge has a chequered design that is iconic among classic cakes.

Battenberg

175g unsalted butter, softened, plus extra for greasing
175g caster sugar
3 eggs
175g self-raising flour, sifted
½ tsp almond extract
pink food-colouring gel
4 tbsp homemade or good-quality apricot jam, sieved
400g yellow marzipan
icing sugar, for dusting the surface

YOU WILL NEED
20cm square, deep cake tin
2-in-1 parchment and foil
cake smoother (optional)

1 Using a double layer of 2-in-1 parchment and foil, fold a barrier to divide the cake tin in half, parchment side upwards. Grease both the base and sides of the tin and the exposed parchment paper.

2 Heat the oven to 180°C/160°C fan/350°F/Gas 4.

3 Cream the butter and sugar together in a stand mixer fitted with the beater, on medium speed for 3–5 minutes, until pale and creamy.

4 Add the eggs, one at a time, beating well between each addition. Add the flour and the almond extract and beat until smooth.

5 Spoon half the mixture into one side of the divided cake tin. Add a few drops of pink food colouring to the remaining mixture in the bowl and mix until you have an even colour. Spoon the pink mixture into the other side of the cake tin.

6 Bake the cakes for 25–30 minutes, until a skewer inserted into the centres comes out clean. Cool in the tin for 10 minutes, then turn out onto a wire rack to cool completely.

7 Place the cooled sponges on a chopping board and, using a ruler, trim the sides of each cake to a make straight edges. Cut each cake in half lengthways to make two pink and two plain sponges. Trim the tops if they are different heights to create four identically shaped sponges.

8 Brush the apricot jam along the long sides of the cakes and join one plain and one pink slice together, lining up the short ends. Then, place one pink and one plain sponge on top, sandwiching them with jam to create a chequered pattern. Brush apricot jam over all the long sides.

Continues overleaf

9 Roll out the marzipan on a work surface lightly dusted with icing sugar to a rectangle measuring about 20 x 30cm. Trim the edges to neaten.

10 Place the chequered cake onto the middle of the marzipan and wrap the marzipan around it, smoothing up the sides and around the corners so that the cake is tightly wrapped (you can use a cake smoother for this, if you have one).

11 To finish, turn the cake over so that the seam is on the underside and trim a thin slice of cake off each end to neaten. Using a sharp knife, score a criss cross pattern in the marzipan on the top of the cake.

Leaving a classic baked cheesecake to cool slowly in the oven will help prevent the top cracking. This one also needs at least 2 hours in the fridge before serving, making it a good prepare-ahead dessert.

Baked Cheesecake

FOR THE BISCUIT BASE
200g digestive biscuits
100g unsalted butter, melted
finely grated zest of
   1 unwaxed lemon

FOR THE FILLING
900g full-fat cream cheese
275g golden caster sugar
40g plain flour, sifted
a pinch of salt
1 tsp lemon juice
3 eggs, plus 2 yolks
300ml soured cream
2 tsp vanilla paste
200g raspberries, to decorate
icing sugar, for dusting

YOU WILL NEED
23cm springform cake tin,
   greased, then base-lined
   with baking paper
large sheet of tin foil (enough
   to cover the base and reach
   above the sides of the tin)
large baking tray half-filled
   with boiling water

1 Heat the oven to 200°C/180°C fan/400°F/Gas 6.

2 Make the biscuit base. Place the biscuits in a freezer bag and bash with a rolling pin to a crumb. Stir in the melted butter and 1 teaspoon of the lemon zest until combined (reserve the remaining lemon zest for the filling).

3 Tip the biscuit mixture into the base of the prepared tin and press down with a spoon. Bake for 10 minutes, then remove from the oven and set aside.

4 Make the filling. Beat the cream cheese in a stand mixer fitted with the beater, on medium speed for 2 minutes, until smooth. Add the sugar, flour and salt and beat on low speed until incorporated.

5 With the mixer on medium speed, add the remaining lemon zest and the lemon juice. Then, add the whole eggs, one at a time, followed by the two yolks, mixing well between each addition. Stir in the soured cream and vanilla.

6 Pour the filling onto the biscuit base and level out. Place the cheesecake on the large sheet of foil and gather up the foil around the sides of the tin (but not over the top).

7 Carefully place the cheesecake and foil into the tray with the boiling water and bake for 15 minutes. Then, reduce the oven to 110°C/90°C fan/225°F/Gas ½ and bake for a further 50 minutes, until the filling is almost set.

8 Turn off the oven and leave the cheesecake to cool and set for 2 hours without opening the oven door. Then, remove from the oven and refrigerate for 2–3 hours, before decorating with raspberries and dusting with icing sugar to serve.

When you get the hang of the two-tone icing technique for these pretty fairy cakes, you can apply it to all manner of cakes – large and small.

Fairy Cakes

FOR THE SPONGE
100g unsalted butter, softened
100g golden caster sugar
1 tsp vanilla paste
2 eggs, beaten
100g self-raising flour, sifted

FOR THE BUTTERCREAM
175g unsalted butter, softened
350g icing sugar, sifted
1 tsp vanilla paste
pink food-colouring gel

YOU WILL NEED
12-hole fairy-cake tin lined
   with 12 fairy-cake cases
large piping bag fitted with
   a large closed star nozzle

1 Heat the oven to 200°C/180°C fan/400°F/Gas 6.

2 Beat together the butter, sugar and vanilla in a stand mixer fitted with the beater, on medium speed for 1–2 minutes, until pale and creamy.

3 With the machine still running, add the beaten eggs, little by little, until fully combined. Reduce the speed to low, and add the flour in two batches, beating until just combined between each addition.

4 Spoon equal amounts of the cake mixture into the cake cases and bake for 12–15 minutes, until golden, springy to the touch, and a skewer inserted into the centres comes out clean. Remove from the oven, place the tray on a wire rack and leave the cakes to cool completely.

5 While the cakes are cooling, make the buttercream. Beat the butter, icing sugar and vanilla in a stand mixer fitted with the beater, on a low speed for 30 seconds, then increase the speed to medium and beat for 1–2 minutes, until pale and creamy.

6 Separate out half the buttercream into a bowl and colour it your chosen shade of pink. Spoon the plain buttercream into the piping bag, keeping it to one side, then spoon the pink buttercream into the other side, trying not to let the buttercreams mix too much.

7 Starting at the centre of each cupcake, pipe a spiral of buttercream working outwards, to cover the whole cake, whipping the piping bag away quickly at the end of the spiral to avoid a tail of icing.

HOW TO...
PIPE A BUTTERCREAM CUPCAKE

Buttercream is the classic cake topping and filling. This vanilla buttercream is ideal for piping. Turn over for some cupcake piping techniques, too.

Vanilla buttercream icing

MAKES ENOUGH FOR 12 CUPCAKES (OR FILLING FOR A 20CM CAKE)
175g unsalted butter, softened
350g icing sugar, sifted
1 tsp vanilla paste

Put the butter, sugar and vanilla in a stand mixer fitted with the beater. Beat on a slow speed for 30 seconds, until combined, then increase the speed to medium and beat for a further 3 minutes, until pale, smooth and fluffy. (The longer you beat it the fluffier it will become.) You may need to stop the mixer to scrape down the bowl from time to time.

Alternatively, you can put the ingredients in a bowl and use an electric hand whisk, or you can beat the buttercream by hand with a wooden spoon – but obviously, it will take you longer to reach the desired consistency by hand.

Storage
The buttercream will keep for up to 3 days in an airtight container, stored in a cool place. It will also freeze well.

COLOURING & FLAVOURING BUTTERCREAM

To flavour or colour buttercream, add your flavouring or colouring drop by tiny drop (a cocktail stick is good for this), stirring to combine between each addition, until you have just the flavour or colour you want. Remember, you can always add more, but you can't take it away again, so be patient.

As well as using shop-bought flavourings, you can flavour buttercream with orange or lemon zest or juice, coffee, cocoa powder, liqueurs, or your favourite fruit purée.

Using a piping bag

Buttercream has to be just the right consistency for piping – too soft and it will not hold its shape; too firm and it will be difficult to achieve an even swirl. Ideally, it should be smooth and velvety with a whippy, fluffy consistency that is firm enough to retain the decoration, and is spreadable. If it is too thick, you could loosen it with a splash of milk; or if too thin, add a little more icing sugar.

There are lots of different shapes and sizes of piping nozzles, giving a range of decorative effects. The most popular are plain, open star and closed top.

For piping cupcakes with a nozzle, use a reuseable piping bag. To clean it after use, simply turn it inside out and pop it in the dishwasher, or wash it by hand in hot, soapy water.

1 Insert the nozzle into the pointed end of the piping bag, ensuring a cosy fit.

2 Fold the top of the piping bag over to make a collar – it will be much easier to fill this way. Spoon the buttercream into the bag so it is about half full, then twist the bag above the buttercream to direct the buttercream towards the nozzle, remove any air and stop it coming out of the bag as you pipe.

3 Use both hands. If you're right-handed, use your right hand to squeeze and your left hand to guide – vice versa if you're left-handed. You may find it easier to stand to gain height over your cake. Hold the piping bag perpendicular to the cake with the nozzle hovering just above, but not touching. Squeeze from the top using even pressure. See over the page for how to create specific effects.

CLASSIC SWIRL

You will need: large or small open star nozzle (depending how tight you want your swirl)

Starting from the centre of the cupcake, pipe a spiral outwards to the edge then, in one smooth, circular motion, work your way inwards to the centre again, slightly overlapping as you go to give height. To finish, stop squeezing when you reach the centre and draw up sharply to form a peak.

PEAKS

You will need: small or medium plain nozzle (depending how large you want your peaks)

Starting from the centre of the cupcake, gently squeeze the bag to form small peaks. Release the pressure and pull the bag away sharply at the end of each squeeze.

ROSE SWIRL

You will need: large closed star nozzle

Starting from the centre of the cupcake, swirl the icing in a smooth, circular motion, spiralling towards the edge, slightly overlapping as you go, until you have covered the cake. Pull away sharply at the end of the spiral.

GEMS

You will need: small, medium or large open star nozzle (depending how large you want your gems)

Starting from the centre of the cupcake, gently squeeze the bag to form small peaks. Release the pressure and pull the bag away sharply at the end of each squeeze.

ROUNDED SWIRL

You will need: medium or large plain nozzle (depending on how tight you want your swirl)

Starting from the centre of the cupcake, pipe a spiral outwards to the edge then, in one smooth, circular motion, work your way inwards to the centre again, slightly overlapping as you go to give height. To finish, stop squeezing when you reach the centre and draw up sharply to form a peak.

FLOWERY SWIRL

You will need: medium or large petal nozzle (depending how tall you want your petals)

Starting from the centre of the cupcake, and with the thinnest part of the nozzle facing upwards, move the piping bag in ever-increasing 'C' shapes, overlapping each C with the next to form the petals around one another (you may find it easier to hold the cupcake in your free hand and turn it using your fingers as you go). Keep working outwards in concentric circles until you have covered the cake.

For a twist on this classic, add 1 teaspoon of ground cinnamon, cardamom or mixed spice to the basic mixture.

Banana Bread

125g unsalted butter
180g light brown soft sugar
2 large eggs, beaten
1 tsp vanilla paste
250g plain flour
1 tsp bicarbonate of soda
½ tsp salt
3 large or 4 medium very ripe
   bananas, well mashed
3 tbsp soured cream

YOU WILL NEED
900g non-stick loaf tin, greased

1 Heat the oven to 180°C/160°C fan/350°F/Gas 4.

2 Beat the butter and sugar together in a stand mixer fitted with the beater, on medium speed for 3–4 minutes, until pale and creamy.

3 Add the eggs, a little at a time, beating well between each addition, until fully combined, then add the vanilla.

4 Sift together the flour, bicarbonate of soda and salt into a bowl. Add one third of the flour mixture, one third of the mashed banana and 1 tablespoon of the soured cream to the creamed butter and sugar mixture and gently beat together. Repeat with another third of flour, banana and soured cream, then finally the remaining third of each.

5 Spoon the mixture into the prepared loaf tin and bake for 1 hour (don't be tempted to open the oven door), until a skewer inserted into the centre comes out clean.

6 Remove the loaf from the oven and leave it to cool in the tin for 15 minutes, then turn it out onto a wire rack to cool completely.

SERVES
16

HANDS-ON
1 HOUR

BAKE
35 MINS

You'll need a cake-decorating turntable to create the spiral effect on the top of this cake, but don't worry if you don't have one – the decoration of real carrots is just as effective without a spiral.

Carrot Cake

FOR THE SPONGE
300g light muscovado sugar
300ml sunflower oil
6 eggs, beaten
225g carrot, grated
180g sultanas
finely grated zest of
    1 unwaxed orange
300g self-raising flour
1½ tsp bicarbonate of soda
2 tsp mixed spice

FOR THE ICING
200g unsalted butter, softened
400g icing sugar, sifted
finely grated zest of
    1 unwaxed orange
1 tsp vanilla paste
175g full-fat cream cheese,
    at room temperature

FOR THE DECORATION
2 tbsp chopped hazelnuts
1 tsp cocoa powder
a few small carrots, green tops
    intact, washed and trimmed

YOU WILL NEED
20cm sandwich tins x 3,
    greased, then lined
    (base and sides)
    with baking paper
cake-decorating
    turntable (optional)
large cranked palette
    knife (optional)

1 Heat the oven to 200°C/180°C fan/400°F/Gas 6.

2 Tip the sugar and oil in a large bowl and mix until the sugar has dissolved in the oil. Whisk in the eggs, then add the carrot, sultanas and orange zest and stir to combine.

3 Sift the flour, bicarbonate of soda and mixed spice together into a bowl, then fold the dry mixture into the wet mixture until no streaks of flour remain. Divide the mixture equally between the three prepared tins.

4 Bake the sponges for 30–35 minutes, until springy to the touch and a skewer inserted into the centres comes out clean. Cool in the tins for 5 minutes, then turn out onto a wire rack to cool completely.

5 Make the icing. Beat the butter, icing sugar, orange zest and vanilla in a stand mixer fitted with the beater, on medium speed for 1–2 minutes, until fluffy. Add the cream cheese and beat for 20–30 seconds more, until smooth and combined.

6 Level the cooled cakes, then place the first layer on a cake plate, and then on a turntable, if using. Spread one quarter of the buttercream over the top of the cake. Top with a second cake, and cover with a further quarter of the buttercream. Finish with the final cake on top.

7 Hold the top of the cake firmly with one hand. Using the cranked palette knife, if you have one, push any excess frosting into the gaps between the layers.

8 Add half the remaining buttercream to the top of the cake and spread it out and down the sides to apply a crumb coat.

Continues overleaf

9 To create the naked effect on the side of the cake, gently smooth the knife around the side to leave only a thin layer of buttercream that shows some of the dark sponge peeping through.

10 Top the cake with the remaining buttercream, using the knife to spread it thickly all the way to the edges.

11 If you're using a turntable, to create the swirl effect, dip the end of the palette knife into the buttercream in the centre of the sponge, then spin the turntable while drawing the knife outwards, using a little pressure to create the spiral. Neaten the frosting around the top edge of the cake.

12 To decorate, in a bowl, combine the nuts and cocoa to create 'soil'. Crumble this over the cake as a patch for the sprouting carrots. Trim the pointed ends off the carrots and press the cut ends down into the patch of 'soil', as if they are coming out of the cake.

We love the summery pink and yellow colours of these classic fondant fancies, but feel free to personalise them using your own favourite icing colours, if you prefer.

Fondant Fancies

FOR THE SPONGE
225g unsalted butter, softened
225g caster sugar
4 eggs
225g self-raising flour, sifted
finely grated zest of
   1 unwaxed lemon

FOR THE BUTTERCREAM
150g unsalted butter, softened
200g icing sugar, sifted
½ tsp vanilla extract

FOR THE MARZIPAN TOPPING
200g natural marzipan
3 tbsp homemade or good-
   quality apricot jam, sieved

**FOR THE ICING &
DECORATION**
1kg ready-to-roll white
   fondant icing
yellow food-colouring gel
pink food-colouring gel
100g icing sugar, sifted
juice of ½ lemon
100g 54% dark chocolate,
   broken into small pieces

YOU WILL NEED
20cm square, deep cake tin,
   greased, then base-lined
   with baking paper
medium piping bag fitted
   with a small plain nozzle
2 small piping bags, each fitted
   with a small writing nozzle

1 Heat the oven to 170°C/150°C fan/325°F/Gas 3.

2 For the sponge, beat the butter, sugar, eggs, flour and lemon zest in a stand mixer fitted with the beater, on medium speed for 2 minutes, until smooth. Tip the mixture into the prepared tin and tap lightly to level out. Bake for about 35–40 minutes, or until a skewer inserted into the centre comes out clean. Leave to cool in the tin for 10 minutes, then turn out onto a wire rack to cool completely. Chill the sponge for 30 minutes.

3 For the buttercream, beat the softened butter, icing sugar and vanilla together in a bowl until pale and fluffy. Place 100g of the buttercream in the medium piping bag and refrigerate to firm up slightly. Reserve the remaining buttercream in the bowl.

4 Roll out the marzipan on a surface lightly dusted with icing sugar to a 20cm square. Remove the chilled cake from the fridge and brush the top with the sieved apricot jam, then place the marzipan on top.

5 Cut the cake into 16 equal squares (each about 4.5cm square). Using the buttercream in the bowl, cover the four sides of each square with buttercream (don't spread it over the marzipan top or the base). Then, using the buttercream in the piping bag, pipe a blob in the centre of the marzipan on top of each square. Leave the cakes to set in the fridge for 20 minutes.

6 For the icing and decoration, cut the fondant icing into small cubes. Place the cubes in a stand mixer fitted with the beater. Mix the fondant on low speed until it starts to break down, adding a splash of water if it's too hard. Very slowly add 150ml of water until the fondant becomes smooth and pourable.

Continues overleaf

7 Divide the pourable fondant into two bowls. Colour one bowl pale yellow and the other bowl pale pink. Be careful not to add too much colouring at once – you can always add more if you want the colour a little darker.

8 Tip the icing sugar into a bowl and add enough lemon juice to form smooth icing of dropping consistency (you may not need all the juice). Spoon the mixture into one of the piping bags fitted with a writing nozzle.

9 Melt the chocolate in a heatproof bowl set over a pan of gently simmering water, stirring occasionally. Once melted, pour the chocolate into the other piping bag fitted with a writing nozzle.

10 Take the cakes out of the fridge and place them on a wire rack set over a roasting tin (to catch the icing). Pour the yellow fondant over eight of the cakes and the pink fondant over the remaining eight cakes.

11 Leave the fondant to set for 5–10 minutes at room temperature, then using the piping bags, pipe the melted chocolate diagonally backwards and forwards over the yellow cakes and the white icing over the pink cakes. Leave to set for 2–3 hours on the wire rack before serving.

If you're catering for the masses, this classic also works well in a standard roasting tin – just make a six-egg mixture and bake it for 40–45 minutes. Drizzle while the cake is warm for the perfect soak.

Lemon Drizzle Traybake

FOR THE SPONGE
225g unsalted butter,
   diced and softened
225g golden caster sugar
275g self-raising flour, sifted
2 tsp baking powder
4 large eggs
50ml whole milk
zest of 3 large or 4 medium
   unwaxed lemons

FOR THE DRIZZLE
juice of 3 large or
   4 medium lemons
150g granulated sugar

TO DECORATE
3 tbsp preserving sugar

YOU WILL NEED
30 x 23cm traybake tin,
   greased, then lined
   (base and sides)
   with baking paper
cocktail stick

1 Heat the oven to 170°C/150°C fan/325°F/Gas 3.

2 Beat together all the sponge ingredients in a stand mixer fitted with the beater, on medium speed for 2 minutes, until smooth.

3 Transfer the mixture to the prepared tin and smooth the top. Bake for 35–40 minutes, until springy to the touch and a skewer inserted into the centre comes out clean. Set aside to cool just a little while you quickly make the drizzle.

4 Stir together the lemon juice and sugar. Using a cocktail stick, poke holes all over the sponge and spoon the drizzle over. Leave the sponge to cool completely in the tin.

5 Sprinkle the traybake with preserving sugar, then remove it from the tin and cut into 24 squares.

This is a quick and easy, classic cherry sponge cake given a little extra texture from the addition of ground almonds. Dusting the cherries with flour helps stop them sinking to the bottom of the cake.

Cherry Cake

200g glacé cherries,
    quartered and rinsed
225g self-raising flour, sifted
175g unsalted butter, softened
175g caster sugar
finely grated zest of
    1 unwaxed lemon
50g ground almonds
3 large eggs

TO DECORATE
175g icing sugar, sifted
juice of 1 lemon
15g flaked almonds, toasted
5 glacé cherries, quartered

YOU WILL NEED
23cm savarin mould
    or bundt tin, greased

1 Heat the oven to 180°C/160°C fan/350°F/Gas 4.

2 Dry the rinsed cherries thoroughly on kitchen paper and toss them in 2 tablespoons of the flour.

3 Put all the remaining sponge ingredients into a large bowl and beat well for 2 minutes to mix thoroughly. Lightly fold in the cherries until evenly distributed, then transfer the mixture to the prepared tin.

4 Bake for 35–40 minutes, until well risen, golden brown and a skewer inserted into the cake comes out clean. Leave to cool in the tin for 10 minutes, then turn out onto a wire rack to cool completely.

5 For the decoration, mix the icing sugar with the lemon juice to a thick paste. Drizzle the paste over the back of a spoon onto the cooled cake, then sprinkle over the toasted almonds and quartered cherries.

Adding the hot coffee to the sponge and icing at the creaming stage helps to dissolve the sugar and lighten the mixture in this classic elevenses treat.

Coffee & Walnut Cake

FOR THE SPONGE
200g unsalted butter, softened
200g golden caster sugar
1 tsp vanilla paste
2 tbsp strong espresso powder
2–3 tbsp boiling water
4 eggs, beaten
200g self-raising flour, sifted
1 tsp baking powder
100g chopped walnuts,
    plus 7 walnut halves
    to decorate

FOR THE BUTTERCREAM
225g unsalted butter, softened
450g icing sugar, sifted
2 tbsp strong espresso powder
2 tbsp boiling water

YOU WILL NEED
20cm sandwich tins x 2,
    greased, then lined
    (base and sides)
    with baking paper
large piping bag fitted with
    a large closed star nozzle

1 Heat the oven to 200°C/180°C fan/400°F/Gas 6.

2 Beat the butter, sugar and vanilla together in a stand mixer fitted with the beater, on medium speed for 1–2 minutes, until pale and creamy.

3 Dissolve the espresso powder in the boiling water, then add this to the creamed butter and beat on medium speed for 1 minute, until fluffy. Add the eggs, a little at a time, beating well between each addition.

4 With the mixer on a low speed, add the flour and baking powder, until just combined. Add the chopped walnuts and mix slowly for a few seconds, until evenly distributed.

5 Divide the mixture equally between the two tins and bake for 25–30 minutes, until a skewer inserted into the centres comes out clean. Leave to cool in the tins for 5 minutes, then turn out onto a wire rack to cool completely.

6 Make the buttercream. Beat the butter and sugar in the bowl of a stand mixer fitted with the beater, on medium speed for 1 minute. Dissolve the espresso powder in the boiling water, then with the mixer on low, add it to the bowl. Increase the speed to medium and cream for 1–2 minutes, until fluffy.

7 To assemble, place one sponge top-side downwards onto a cake plate and spread with one third of the buttercream. Top with the second sponge, and use another third to cover.

8 Spoon the remaining buttercream into the piping bag fitted with the star nozzle. Pipe six swirls of buttercream around the top edge of the cake and one swirl in the centre. Top each swirl with a walnut half.

Cakes don't get much simpler than this one. Cool it in the tin to allow the sponge to soak up all the gooey syrup. For an alternative, try replacing the vanilla with 1 tablespoon of ground ginger.

Pineapple Upside-down Cake

8 tinned pineapple rings
   in natural juice, drained
200g golden syrup
7 glacé cherries, halved
200g unsalted butter
200g caster sugar
200g self-raising flour, sifted
¾ tsp baking powder
3 large eggs
75ml whole milk
1½ tsp vanilla extract

YOU WILL NEED
20cm solid-based, round cake
   tin, greased, then base-lined
   with baking paper

1 Heat the oven to 180°C/160°C fan/350°F/Gas 4. Halve six of the drained pineapple rings and quarter the remaining two. Set aside.

2 Pour the golden syrup into the prepared tin, tilting the tin to evenly spread the syrup. Arrange the pineapple halves in a circle around the edge of the tin and arrange the pineapple quarters in the middle. Place a glacé cherry in the middle of each pineapple half and one cherry in the middle.

3 Place the butter, sugar, flour and baking powder in the bowl of a food processor. Lightly beat the eggs, milk and vanilla extract together in a jug, then add the mixture to the processor bowl. Blitz for 1 minute, until thoroughly blended.

4 Spoon the mixture into the tin and level out with a palette knife. Bake for 35–45 minutes, until golden and a skewer inserted into the centre comes out clean. Leave the cake to cool in the tin for at least 15 minutes, then turn out onto a serving plate or chopping board and cut into slices.

Parkin is a sticky cake flavoured with syrupy molasses, oatmeal and ginger, traditionally enjoyed on Bonfire Night in the north of England. Like a fine wine, parkin improves with age, so bake it up to a week before you want to eat it.

Parkin

1 large egg, beaten
4 tbsp whole milk
200g unsalted butter
100g molasses or treacle
200g golden syrup
50g dark brown soft sugar
100g medium oatmeal
250g self-raising flour, sifted
1 tbsp ground ginger
1 tsp mixed spice

YOU WILL NEED
20cm square cake tin, greased, then lined (base and sides) with baking paper

1 Heat the oven to 160°C/140°C fan/315°F/Gas 2–3.

2 Beat the egg and milk together in a jug.

3 Place the butter in a large pan with the molasses or treacle, golden syrup and sugar. Melt everything together over a low heat, stirring occasionally.

4 Remove the pan from the heat and stir in the oatmeal, flour, ginger and mixed spice. Add the egg and milk mixture and stir until well combined.

5 Pour the mixture into the prepared tin and bake for 50 minutes to 1 hour, until the sponge is firm to the touch, but not dry. Leave the sponge in the tin until completely cold, then wrap it (still in the tin) in baking paper and foil. Store for a week, then turn out and cut into 16 squares. Eat within 2 weeks.

This is Prue's take on the retro English angel cake. The pretty decoration is super-easy: a cocktail stick and stripes of pink icing are all you need.

Angel Cake Slices

FOR THE GÉNOISE
60g unsalted butter,
    melted and cooled,
    plus extra for greasing
4 large eggs, at room
    temperature
120g caster sugar
120g plain flour, sifted
½ tsp vanilla extract
½ tsp natural raspberry
    flavouring
pink food-colouring gel
finely grated zest of
    1 small unwaxed lemon
yellow food-colouring gel

**FOR THE ITALIAN MERINGUE
BUTTERCREAM**
100g caster sugar
1 large egg white
85g unsalted butter, softened

FOR THE FONDANT ICING
250g fondant icing sugar
pink food-colouring gel

YOU WILL NEED
2-in-1 parchment and foil cut
    to a rectangle of 50 x 20cm
33 x 25cm traybake tin
sugar thermometer
small piping bag fitted with
    a medium writing nozzle
cocktail stick

1 For the génoise, fold the foiled parchment to divide the cake tin into three even sections (each measuring 20 x 10cm) with the parchment side facing upwards, and grease with melted butter. Heat the oven to 190°C/170°C fan/375°F/Gas 5.

2 Tip the eggs and sugar into a bowl set over a pan of gently simmering water. Gently whisk until the sugar has dissolved and the mixture reaches 43°C/109°F on the sugar thermometer.

3 Weigh the mixture in the bowl of a stand mixer, then record the weight. Attach the bowl to the mixer and, using the whisk attachment, whisk the mixture until it is thick and mousse-like, and leaves a ribbon trail when you lift the whisk.

4 Meanwhile, divide the flour evenly between three small bowls. Do the same for the butter. Stir the vanilla into one bowl of butter. Stir the raspberry flavouring and a small drop of pink food colouring into the second bowl of butter, and the lemon zest and a small drop of yellow food colouring into the third.

5 Divide the whisked egg mixture into three bowls. Working with one bowl of egg mixture, flour and butter at a time, sift the flour over the egg mixture and gently fold in. Add the butter and fold – work quickly to prevent the mixture collapsing.

6 Repeat Step 5 with the remaining bowls of egg mixture, flour and butter to give three mixtures – vanilla, raspberry and lemon. Pour each into a section of the cake tin and bake for 12–15 minutes, until the tops spring back when pressed. Cool a little in the tin, then transfer to a wire rack to cool completely.

7 For the Italian meringue buttercream, melt the sugar in 3 tablespoons of water very gently in a pan over a low heat. Meanwhile, whisk the egg white in the clean bowl of a stand mixer fitted with a whisk, to soft peaks. Once the sugar has completely dissolved, increase the heat to a rapid boil until the syrup reaches 121°C/250°F on a sugar thermometer.

Continues overleaf

8 Remove the pan from the heat. With the whisk at full speed, slowly pour the hot syrup onto the egg whites in a thin stream. Continue whisking until the meringue is very thick and glossy and has cooled to room temperature.

9 Gradually add the butter, whisking after each addition until the buttercream is smooth and thick. Chill until firm.

10 To assemble, trim the sponges so they are identical in size and height. Spread half the buttercream over the vanilla sponge and top with the raspberry sponge. Spread the other half of the buttercream over the raspberry sponge and top with the lemon sponge (you might not need all the buttercream).

11 For the fondant icing, sift the icing sugar into a bowl and add 1½–2 tablespoons of water to mix to a stiff, dropping consistency. Spoon one quarter of the icing into a small bowl and colour it pink. Spoon the pink icing into the piping bag fitted with a writing nozzle.

12 Spread the white fondant icing over the top (not the sides) of the lemon sponge. Pipe fine lines of icing across the width of the cake, spacing them 1cm apart. Using a cocktail stick, gently drag the icing lines in opposite directions through the white fondant to feather. Cut the cake into six even slices and serve.

Madeira cake is not named after the islands, but for the fortified Portuguese wine that comes from them. The association is fitting because, like the cake, Madeira wine is baked in an oven.

Madeira Cake

FOR THE SPONGE
150g unsalted butter, softened
150g caster sugar
4 eggs, beaten
200g self-raising flour, sifted
a pinch of salt
finely grated zest of
    2 unwaxed oranges
finely grated zest of
    1 large unwaxed lemon

FOR THE CANDIED PEEL
rind of 1 unwaxed orange,
    cut into matchsticks
rind of 1 unwaxed lemon,
    cut into matchsticks
75g caster sugar

FOR THE ICING
150g icing sugar, sifted
juice of ½–1 lemon

YOU WILL NEED
900g loaf tin, greased,
    then dusted with flour

1 Heat the oven to 180°C/160°C fan/350°F/Gas 4.

2 Beat the butter and sugar in a stand mixer fitted with the beater, on medium speed for 5 minutes, until pale and creamy.

3 Add the eggs, a little at a time, beating well between each addition. Add the flour, salt, and orange and lemon zests and beat until smooth.

4 Spoon the mixture into the prepared tin and level with a palette knife. Bake for 55 minutes to 1 hour, until a skewer inserted into the centre comes out clean. Cool in the tin for 15 minutes, then transfer to a wire rack to cool completely.

5 Meanwhile, make the candied peel. Bring a large pan of water to the boil, add the matchsticks of orange and lemon peel. Boil for 15 seconds, then drain through a sieve. Return the peel to the pan and add the sugar and 75ml of water. Bring to the boil and boil for 8–10 minutes, until the liquid is syrupy. Remove the peel from the pan and place it on a wire rack to cool.

6 For the icing, mix the icing sugar and lemon juice together to form a thick paste (you may not need all the juice).

7 Once the cake is cool, pour the icing over the top of the cake and scatter the candied peel on top.

Baked in just 10 minutes, this classic is delicious rolled with homemade jam or curd, and sublime with cream, too. As it is a fatless sponge, it doesn't store particularly well, so eat it on the day you make it.

Swiss Roll

3 eggs, at room temperature
75g caster sugar, plus extra
   for sprinkling
75g plain flour
a pinch of salt
6 tbsp homemade or
   good-quality fruit jam
   or curd
200ml whipping cream,
   whipped to soft peaks

YOU WILL NEED
20 x 30cm Swiss roll tin,
   greased, then lined
   with baking paper
35cm-long sheet of
   baking paper

1 Heat the oven to 220°C/200°C fan/425°F/Gas 7.

2 Whisk the eggs and sugar in a stand mixer fitted with a whisk, on high speed until the mixture is thick and mousse-like, and leaves a ribbon trail when you lift the whisk.

3 Sift the flour and salt onto a sheet of baking paper, then sift half of it over the egg mixture. Fold it in with a metal spoon, then sift in the remaining flour and salt and fold until the mixture is smooth and streak-free. Gently scrape down the sides of the bowl and check the bottom of the mixture for any pockets of flour – incorporate them if you find them.

4 Pour the mixture into the prepared tin and gently tip the tin so that the mixture flows into the corners and is level. Bake for 9–10 minutes, until golden brown and springy to the touch.

5 Lay the sheet of baking paper on the work surface and sprinkle with caster sugar. As soon as you take the sponge out of the oven turn it out onto the sugar-coated paper – lift off the tin and peel away the baking paper that had lined the tin.

6 Turn the sponge so that one of the short ends is closest to you. Using a sharp knife, score a cut 2cm in from the short end – this will help the roll. Starting from that end, gently roll up the Swiss roll with the sheet of paper rolled inside. Place the roll on a wire rack and leave to cool completely.

7 To assemble, gently unroll the roll and trim off the edges with a sharp knife. Spread with jam or fruit curd leaving a 2cm border around the edge. Cover the jam with a layer of whipped cream, keeping the 2cm border.

8 Starting again at the scored end of the roll, gently roll up, this time without the baking paper. Turn the roll seam-side downwards and sprinkle with caster sugar before serving.

This cheery, red, American classic is traditionally baked for Christmas and Valentine's Day – but really it suits any occasion. If you wish you could leave the sides of the cake naked or semi-naked.

Red Velvet Cake

FOR THE SPONGE
375g unsalted butter, softened
325g golden caster sugar
4 eggs, beaten
3 tbsp cocoa powder
2 tsp vanilla extract
2 tbsp red food-colouring paste
100ml hot water
350ml buttermilk
1 tsp salt
450g self-raising flour, sifted
1½ tsp white vinegar
1½ tsp bicarbonate of soda

FOR THE BUTTERCREAM
250g unsalted butter, softened
2 tsp vanilla paste
500g icing sugar, sifted
200g full-fat cream cheese,
    at room temperature

YOU WILL NEED
20cm sandwich tins x 3,
    greased then lined
    (base and sides)
    with baking paper

1 Heat the oven to 200°C/180°C fan/400°F/Gas 6.

2 Beat the butter and sugar in a stand mixer fitted with the beater, on medium speed for 2–3 minutes, until pale and creamy. Add the eggs, a little at a time, beating well between each addition until combined.

3 In a small bowl or jug, mix the cocoa powder, vanilla, red food-colouring and hot water together to form a paste. Add this to the cake mixture and mix well until combined.

4 Combine the buttermilk and salt in a jug. Add one third to the bowl with the cake mixture, then add one third of the flour. Alternate buttermilk and flour, until everything is combined.

5 In a small bowl, mix the vinegar and bicarbonate of soda together and add to the cake mixture. Beat until smooth.

6 Divide the mixture equally between the prepared tins and bake for 20–25 minutes, until springy to the touch and a skewer inserted into the centres comes out clean. Cool in the tins for 5 minutes, then turn out onto a wire rack to cool completely.

7 To make the buttercream, beat the butter and vanilla in a stand mixer fitted with the beater, on high speed for about 1 minute, until smooth and fluffy.

8 Add the icing sugar, one quarter at a time, beating between each addition slowly at first, then on high speed for about 1 minute. With the mixer on low, add the cream cheese and beat briefly, until smooth.

9 To assemble, level the sponges, keeping any offcuts for decoration. Smear a little buttercream onto a cake plate and top with the first sponge.

Continues overleaf

10 Spread over one quarter of the buttercream, overhanging the edge a little, then top with a second sponge. Spread with another quarter – again, leave an overhang. Top with the remaining sponge.

11 With a palette knife, spread the overhanging buttercream all around the side of the cake, to seal and neaten.

12 Next, using one third of the remaining buttercream, spread a thin, even layer over the top of the cake.

13 Clean the palette knife and smooth off any excess buttercream to create a crumb coat. Chill the cake for at least 30 minutes to firm up, then add a second, slightly thicker coat using the remaining buttercream.

14 To decorate the cake, crumble the reserved offcuts of cake, then sprinkle these neatly around the edge of the top of the cake.

CHAPTER TWO

Chocolate

The secret to a great chocolate cake is not to overbake it – when you insert the skewer it's okay if it comes out a little pasty (but not wet). A gooey cake will last you a few days without going dry.

Ultimate Chocolate Cake

FOR THE SPONGE
280g 70% dark chocolate, broken into pieces
280g unsalted butter, softened
325g light muscovado sugar
2 tsp vanilla paste
4 eggs, plus 4 egg yolks, beaten together
200g soured cream
1 tsp baking powder
50g cocoa powder, sifted
250g self-raising flour, sifted

FOR THE BUTTERCREAM
150g dark chocolate chips
250g unsalted butter, softened
500g icing sugar, sifted
75g soured cream

YOU WILL NEED
20cm springform tins x 2, greased, then lined (base and sides) with baking paper
large piping bag fitted with a medium petal nozzle

1 Heat the oven to 180°C/160°C fan/350°F/Gas 4.

2 Make the sponge. Melt the chocolate in a bowl set over a pan of simmering water. Remove from the heat and leave to cool.

3 Beat the butter, sugar and vanilla in a stand mixer fitted with the beater, on medium speed for about 5 minutes, until pale and creamy. Reduce the speed to low and add the eggs, a little at a time, beating well between each addition. If the mixture begins to curdle add 1 tablespoon of the flour and mix again.

4 With the mixer on low speed, pour in the cooled, melted chocolate, then the soured cream. Mix to combine, then add the baking powder, cocoa powder and flour, one third at a time, mixing between each addition until just combined.

5 Divide the mixture equally between the prepared tins. Bake for 35–45 minutes, until a skewer inserted into the centres comes out pasty. Put the tins on a wire rack and leave to cool.

6 Make the buttercream. Melt the chocolate chips in a bowl set over a pan of simmering water. Remove from the heat and leave to cool.

7 Beat the butter and icing sugar in a stand mixer fitted with the beater on medium speed for 3–5 minutes, until pale and creamy, then add the cooled, melted chocolate and soured cream. Beat for 1 minute, until smooth.

8 Once the cakes are cool, cut each cake in half horizontally. Place one sponge, top-side downwards on a plate. Transfer one third of the buttercream to the piping bag and set aside. Spread one third of the remaining buttercream over the top of the cake, then top with the next sponge. Repeat twice more to sandwich all the layers, then top with the final sponge. Pipe buttercream petals from the centre outwards, to cover the cake.

SCALING QUANTITIES
ULTIMATE CHOCOLATE CAKE

Use this table to adjust your chocolate cake mixture according to the size or shape of cake you want to make. The quantities for the 25cm and 30cm round cakes are for two 5cm-deep cake tins. If you have only one tin, bake in two batches (half quantities for each batch), making one sponge, then repeating for a second. The buttercream quantities will fill and top the round cakes, and top the loaf and traybake.

	25cm round, deep cake tin	30cm round, deep cake tin	900g loaf tin	23 x 30cm traybake tin
For the chocolate sponge				
70% dark chocolate, broken into pieces	430g	630g	170g	280g
unsalted butter, softened	430g	630g	170g	280g
light muscovado sugar	500g	730g	200g	325g
vanilla paste	4 tsp	6 tsp	1 tsp	2 tsp
eggs	6	10	3	4
egg yolks	6	8	2	4
soured cream	320g	450g	120g	200g
baking powder	3 tsp	4 tsp	1 tsp	1 tsp
cocoa powder, sifted	80g	110g	30g	50g
self-raising flour, sifted	400g	560g	150g	250g
For the chocolate buttercream				
dark chocolate chips	200g	300g	75g	100g
unsalted butter, softened	400g	500g	150g	200g
icing sugar, sifted	800g	1kg	300g	400g
soured cream	100g	140g	35g	50g
Baking time @ 180°C/ 160°C fan/350°F/Gas 4	45–55 mins	50 mins– 1 hour	1 hour	45–55 mins

A classic roulade is made without flour, making it gluten-free. Add berries to the whipped cream filling, or ripple the cream with chocolate hazelnut spread or dulce de leche for a decadent dessert.

Chocolate Roulade

175g 70% dark chocolate, broken into small pieces
6 large eggs, separated
175g caster sugar
1 tbsp cocoa powder
300ml double cream, whipped to soft peaks
icing sugar, for dusting

YOU WILL NEED
20 x 30cm Swiss roll tin, greased, then lined with baking paper
35cm-long sheet of baking paper

1 Heat the oven to 180°C/160°C fan/350°F/Gas 4. Melt the chocolate in a bowl set over a pan of simmering water. Stir until smooth, then remove from the heat and cool slightly.

2 Whisk the eggs yolks and sugar in a stand mixer fitted with the whisk, on high speed until the mixture is thick and mousse-like, and leaves a ribbon trail when you lift the whisk.

3 In a separate, clean, grease-free bowl, whisk the egg whites to stiff (but not dry) peaks.

4 Pour the chocolate mixture into the egg-yolk mixture and fold together with a large metal spoon. Add 1 large spoonful of egg whites and fold to loosen.

5 Carefully fold in the remaining egg whites, then sift the cocoa powder over the top and fold until completely combined.

6 Pour the mixture into the prepared tin and gently tip the tin so that the mixture flows into the corners and is level. Bake for 20–25 minutes, until risen and slightly crisp. Remove from the oven and leave on a wire rack to cool in the tin.

7 Lay the sheet of baking paper on the work surface and sprinkle with icing sugar. Turn out the roulade onto the sugar-coated paper. Peel away the baking paper that was lining the tin.

8 Turn the roulade so that one of the short ends is closest to you. Using a sharp knife, score a shallow cut 2cm in from the closest short end. Spread the roulade with the cream leaving a 2cm border around the edge. Using the paper to help, gently roll up the roulade. (It's normal for the roulade to crack.)

9 Roll until the join is underneath, then transfer to a serving plate and dust with icing sugar before serving.

This spectacular snake cake is sure to cause a sensation at any birthday party. The netting from a bag of shop-bought citrus fruit provides the perfect template for the scaly skin..

Snakey Birthday Cakey

FOR THE SPONGE
300ml boiling water
100g 70% dark chocolate,
    very finely chopped
1 tsp bicarbonate of soda
200g unsalted butter, softened
350g golden caster sugar
250g condensed milk
20 drops of orange oil
finely grated zest of
    1 unwaxed orange
2 tbsp glycerine
4 large eggs, beaten
400g extra-fine sponge flour
4 tsp baking powder
50g cocoa
½ tsp fine salt

FOR THE FONDANT ICING
85ml chilled water
24g gelatine powder
200g liquid glucose
4 tbsp glycerine
1.35kg icing sugar, sifted
light green food-colouring gel
dark green food-colouring gel
red food-colouring gel
yellow food-colouring gel

**FOR THE CHOCOLATE
MERINGUE BUTTERCREAM**
150g 70% dark chocolate
4 large egg whites
220g caster sugar
160g unsalted butter,
    diced, softened

**FOR THE CRISPED-RICE
SCULPTURE**
25g unsalted butter
100g white marshmallows
75g crisped rice cereal

Continues overleaf

1 Heat the oven to 180°C/160°C fan/350°F/Gas 4.

2 For the sponge, pour the boiling water into a jug, add the chocolate and stir to melt, then stir in the bicarbonate of soda.

3 Beat the butter, sugar, condensed milk, orange oil and orange zest in a stand mixer fitted with the beater, on medium speed for 1 minute, until smooth. With the mixer still running, add the glycerine and eggs, and mix until well combined.

4 In a separate bowl, sift together the flour, baking powder, cocoa and salt. With the mixer on medium speed, add half the flour mixture and mix until combined, then add the watery chocolate mixture, then the remaining flour mixture and combine for 1–2 minutes to a smooth batter.

5 Fill the two cupcake cases three-quarters full, then divide the remaining batter evenly between the two cake tins. Bake the cupcakes for 25–30 minutes and the cakes for 40–45 minutes, until a skewer inserted into the centres comes out clean. Leave to cool in the tins for 5 minutes, then transfer to a wire rack to cool completely.

6 For the fondant, pour the cold water into a small bowl, then sprinkle over the gelatine and leave for 3 minutes, until bloomed.

7 In a small pan simmer the glucose for 30 seconds, then add the gelatine and glycerine, stirring until dissolved. Tip the icing sugar into a bowl and pour in the glucose mixture. Mix with a spatula, then bring everything together with your hands and knead it gently to a smooth fondant. Wrap the icing in cling film and set aside.

8 For the chocolate meringue buttercream, melt the chocolate in a bowl set over a pan of gently simmering water. Stir, then remove from the heat and leave to cool.

Continues overleaf

Chocolate **83**

1 packet snake sweets
pink edible lustre spray
gold edible lustre spray

YOU WILL NEED
6- or 12-hole muffin tray,
   lined with 2 cupcake cases
23cm deep, springform cake tins
   x 2, greased, then base-lined
   with baking paper
large piping bag fitted with
   a large plain nozzle
5cm round cutter
cocktail sticks
cake-decorating paintbrush
netting from a bag of citrus fruit

9 Place the egg whites and sugar in a bowl set over a pan of simmering water and stir to dissolve the sugar. Pour the mixture into a stand mixer fitted with a whisk and whisk to a thick, glossy meringue. Whisk in the cooled, melted chocolate, then add the butter, little by little, and whisk to a smooth, fluffy buttercream. Spoon half the mixture into the piping bag and set aside.

10 To assemble, carve the round cakes to become the main body of the snake, sitting one on top of the other. Using the 5cm round cutter, cut out the centre of the cake, leaving a hole in the middle. Sandwich the cakes together with some of the buttercream in the bowl, then cover the cake in a crumb coat and chill for 20 minutes.

11 Hollow out the two cupcakes and fill them with snake sweets. Stick them together with some of the buttercream in the bowl, then carve them to make an egg shape. Cover in a thin layer of buttercream to give a crumb coat and chill for 20 minutes.

12 For the crisped-rice sculpture, place the butter and marshmallows in a pan over a low heat, stirring until melted. Remove from the heat and stir in the crisped rice and mix until coated. Chill to a moulding consistency (about 30 minutes).

13 Once mouldable, wet your hands and use some of the crisped rice to shape a little tail that sticks up, and the remainder to create a head shape that fits to the top of the cake. Place the pieces on a plate and chill to firm up.

14 Remove the cake from the fridge and use a cocktail stick to secure the tail to the bottom end of the snake shape, then pipe the buttercream all over the cake. Smooth over with a palette knife and chill again for 20 minutes.

15 While the cake is chilling, colour two-thirds of the fondant light green. On a surface lightly dusted with icing sugar, roll out two-thirds of the green fondant to a large circle, big enough to cover the cake, reserving the remaining green fondant for the head.

16 Carefully cover the cake with the circle of green fondant, moulding it between the two cakes to form the coils. Using a cake-decorating paintbrush with some watered-down green food colouring, paint along the creases of the snake coils to make a shadow.

17 Lay the citrus-bag netting over the cake and spray the fondant with pink and gold lustre spray to create a scale effect.

18 Roll out half the remaining white fondant and use this to cover the cupcake 'egg'. Use the netting again as a template and spray with gold lustre spray. Using the white fondant trimmings, shape the snake's teeth – mould them around the tips of a few cocktail sticks and pinch the ends to create the points.

19 Roll out the remaining green fondant and use this to cover the snake's head.

20 Colour half the remaining white fondant dark green and the other half red, reserving a marble-sized piece of white fondant to colour yellow.

21 Roll out the dark green fondant and cut out pieces for around the eyes and for the collar. Make two eyes out of a little bit of red and yellow fondant and stick them in place with water, then add the green pieces round the eyes.

22 Roll out the remaining red fondant and use this to line the inside of the mouth, keeping a little back to make the tongue. Insert cocktail sticks halfway into the back of the head and attach the head to the main cake, then use water to stick on the fondant collar pieces to hide the join.

23 Insert the teeth into the snake's head, then make a red tongue with the reserved red fondant and stick it in the mouth. Fill the inside coil of the cake with the remaining buttercream and place the egg on top.

16   **1½** HOURS   **20** MINS

Andrew's hazelnuts dipped in caramel (from Series 7) may seem an effort, but they are worth it – not only do they look impressive, they give a crunch to each slice.

Andrew

Orange, Salted Caramel & Chocolate Mirror Glaze Cake

FOR THE GÉNOISE
5 eggs
165g caster sugar
165g plain flour
finely grated zest of 2 large
    unwaxed oranges
a pinch of salt
40g unsalted butter, melted,
    plus extra for greasing

FOR THE SALTED
CARAMEL SAUCE
55g unsalted butter
130g light muscovado sugar
600ml double cream
1 tsp crushed sea salt

FOR THE CHOCOLATE
MIRROR GLAZE
150ml double cream
135g caster sugar
55g cocoa powder
3 gelatine leaves

TO DECORATE
50g granulated sugar
8 blanched hazelnuts
chocolate curls (optional)

YOU WILL NEED
20cm springform tins x 2,
    greased, then base-lined
    with baking paper
20cm cake card
cocktail sticks or
    wooden skewers
newspaper sheets,
    to protect the floor

1 Heat the oven to 180°C/160°C Fan/350°F/Gas 4.

2 For the génoise, whisk the eggs and sugar in a stand mixer and fitted with the whisk, on high speed until the mixture is thick and mousse-like and leaves a ribbon trail when you lift the whisk.

3 Sift the flour into the mixture one third at a time, gently folding in each batch before adding the next. Fold in the orange zest and salt. Slowly pour the melted butter down the side of the bowl and fold in with a large metal spoon.

4 Divide the mixture equally between the prepared cake tins, and bake for 18–20 minutes, or until a skewer inserted in the centres comes out clean. Cool in the tins for 5 minutes, then transfer to a wire rack to cool completely.

5 For the salted caramel sauce, place the butter and sugar in a small pan over a low heat and stir for 3–4 minutes, until the sugar has melted. Drizzle in 75ml of the double cream, mixing well. Bring to a simmer for 1 minute, then remove from the heat. Stir in the sea salt and set aside, stirring occasionally, until cool.

6 Using an electric hand whisk, whisk the remaining 525ml of double cream until it forms soft peaks, then gently whisk in the cooled salted caramel.

7 To assemble the cake, using a large serrated knife, cut each cake in half horizontally to make four layers. Carefully place the first layer on the cake card. Using a palette knife, spread about a 5mm layer of cream on top. Top with a layer of sponge and repeat the cream and cake layers until you have four layers of génoise with salted caramel cream on top of each layer.

Continues overleaf

8 Using a palette knife, apply a thin crumb coat of cream all over the cake, filling any gaps to give a smooth surface. Chill for 20 minutes.

9 Reserve about 5 tablespoons of the cream for decoration, then add a thick layer of cream all over the cake, smoothing neatly. Chill for 20 minutes, until the cream is firm.

10 For the chocolate mirror glaze, place the cream, sugar, cocoa powder and 150ml of water in a small pan and heat gently, stirring to dissolve the sugar. Bring to a simmer for 2 minutes, then remove from the heat and leave to cool for 10 minutes.

11 Soak the gelatine leaves in cold water for 5 minutes. Squeeze any excess water from the leaves and stir them into the glaze until dissolved. Pass the glaze through a fine sieve into a measuring jug and tap on a hard surface to remove any air bubbles. Leave to cool until thick, like pourable custard.

12 Transfer the cake to a wire rack set over a large baking tray. Pour the glaze evenly over the top and down the sides of the cake. Chill the cake for 1 hour to set the glaze.

13 To decorate, put the sugar and 2 tablespoons of water in a small pan over a medium heat. Swirl the pan to help the sugar caramelise but do not stir. Heat for 3–4 minutes, until the sugar is an amber colour, then remove from the heat.

14 Attach each hazelnut to the end of a cocktail stick or wooden skewer. Very carefully dip each hazelnut into the caramel and hang it over the edge of a work surface, using a heavy chopping board to hold the sticks in place (protect the floor with newspaper). Once you've coated all the hazelnuts, use scissors to trim the caramel spikes to the same length and remove the nuts from the sticks onto a sheet of baking paper.

15 Place the cake on a serving plate and pipe 8 small circles of salted caramel cream around the edge. Put a caramelised hazelnut on each circle. Pile chocolate curls in the centre, if using.

These small but perfectly formed cakes are traditionally made with ground almonds, but in this recipe the hazelnuts, once combined with the browned butter, add an irresistible depth. This recipe is quick to make – you can have a tempting batch of financiers ready within 30 minutes.

Hazelnut & Chocolate Financiers

70g unsalted butter, diced
70g golden caster sugar
60g ground hazelnuts
30g cocoa powder
25g plain flour, sifted
25g runny honey
80g egg white

TO DECORATE
50g chocolate hazelnut
    spread, melted
25g chopped hazelnuts

YOU WILL NEED
medium disposable
    piping bag (optional)
16-hole silicone mould
    (shape of your choice),
    or a greased, non-stick
    12-hole muffin tray

1 Heat the oven to 220°C/200°C fan/425°F/Gas 7.

2 Melt the diced butter in a small pan over a medium–high heat for 5–10 minutes, until it starts to turn brown at the bottom and smells like popcorn. Remove from the heat and set aside.

3 In a bowl whisk together the sugar, ground hazelnuts, cocoa powder and flour. Add the honey and egg white and whisk until well combined.

4 Pour the melted brown butter into the bowl with the sugar mixture and whisk again until completely combined.

5 Spoon the mixture into the piping bag, if using, and snip a 1cm hole in the end. Pipe equal amounts of the mixture into the holes in your silicone mould or greased muffin tray. Alternatively, simply spoon in the mixture in equal amounts.

6 Bake the financiers for 10–15 minutes, until a skewer inserted into the centres comes out clean. Remove the tray from the oven and place it on a wire rack to allow the cakes to cool (about 10–15 minutes).

7 Use a teaspoon to drizzle each financier with a little melted hazelnut spread and sprinkle over a few chopped hazelnuts.

HOW TO...
DECORATE WITH CHOCOLATE

The first and most important rule for decorating with chocolate is that whatever chocolate you're using – white, milk or dark – always use the best quality available.

MELTING CHOCOLATE

Melt chocolate slowly using a low heat. Overheated chocolate can scorch and separate or, in the case of milk or white chocolate, turn grainy or lumpy – this is technically known as 'seizing' (white chocolate is particularly sensitive to heat). There are two ways to melt chocolate: in a bowl over a pan of water or in a microwave.

METHOD 1 Break the chocolate into small, even-sized pieces and place the pieces in a heatproof bowl. Set the bowl over a pan that is one third full with gently simmering or steaming water, making sure that the bottom of the bowl doesn't touch the water. Turn the heat to low, or turn it off completely, and just let the chocolate melt, occasionally giving it a stir to help it, if you like. When it's melted carefully lift the bowl off the pan.

METHOD 2 Break the chocolate into pieces as for method 1. Microwave dark chocolate on 50-per-cent power in 30-second bursts, until melted. Stir the chocolate between each burst. Microwave milk and white chocolate in the same way, but at 30-per-cent power.

TEMPERING CHOCOLATE

Tempering chocolate is a process of heating and cooling chocolate to a particular temperature (you'll need a sugar thermometer) to produce chocolate that is shiny and has a good snap. It is perfect for coating cakes, or making chocolate decorations and filled chocolates.

There are two basic ways to temper chocolate:

METHOD 1 Follow the process for melting chocolate, opposite. Melt two thirds of the chocolate until a sugar thermometer reaches 45°C/113°F for dark chocolate or 43°C/109°F for milk or white. Remove from the heat, then stir in the remaining third of chocolate until melted. Leave to cool, continuing to stir, until the temperature reaches 27°C/80°F.

METHOD 2 Follow the process for melting chocolate, opposite. Melt all the chocolate until a sugar thermometer reaches 45°C/113°F for dark chocolate or 43°C/109°F for milk or white. Remove from the heat and pour two-thirds of the melted chocolate onto a dry marble slab or work surface. With a spatula or palette knife, work the chocolate by spreading it back and forth until it thickens and becomes difficult to spread. Scrape this into the remaining melted chocolate and stir. Gently reheat the chocolate until it reaches 31°C/88°F for dark chocolate or 27°C/81°F for milk or white.

MAKING CHOCOLATE GANACHE

Ganache is a combination of dark chocolate and double cream and is perfect for filling or icing cakes – or for making rich chocolate truffles. A ganache will keep in the fridge for up to 1 week.

The rule of thumb for a soft ganache icing is to use one part dark chocolate to two parts double cream. For a cake filling, use equal weights of chocolate and double cream.

1 Break the chocolate into small, even-sized pieces and place it in a heatproof bowl.

2 Heat the cream in a pan over a low–medium heat to just below boiling point, then pour it into the bowl over the chocolate.

3 Stir until the chocolate melts, then set aside to cool and thicken before use. Alternatively, once the ganache is cool, whisk it with an electric hand whisk until light, creamy and mousse-like.

Making chocolate decorations

For the best results, use tempered chocolate (see page 93) for making chocolate decorations, although simple melted chocolate can work, too.

CURLS

Pour the tempered or melted chocolate onto a marble slab, work surface or baking sheet. Spread the chocolate as smoothly as possible into a thin, even layer using a flexible spatula or palette knife. Leave the chocolate to cool at room temperature, until nearly set. Then, as soon as the chocolate is firm but still pliable, scrape the edge of a palette knife away from you at a 45-degree angle to roll the chocolate into cylinders or curls.

LEAVES

Using a small brush, paint the underside of washed and dried rose leaves (leave a little bit of stem to help with the peeling later), or other edible leaves, with a layer (or several layers) of tempered chocolate. Place the coated leaves on baking paper and leave to cool and set, then, starting at the stem end, carefully peel away the leaf from the chocolate. Attach the chocolate leaves to cakes or chocolate flowers with a little melted chocolate, royal icing or edible glue.

PIPED DECORATIONS

Tempered chocolate can be piped onto baking paper, non-stick acetate or a silicone mat into the decorative shape of your choice, including words, trees, flowers, hearts, spirals or swirls.

Fill a small disposable piping bag with tempered chocolate and snip off the tip, then pipe your design on a sheet of baking paper or acetate. (Either pipe the chocolate freehand or draw a template on a piece of paper, then place it under the baking paper or acetate to follow as you pipe.)

Leave the chocolate to set firmly at room temperature or in the fridge. Then, peel the designs off the paper or acetate with a palette knife and use straightaway, or store layered between sheets of baking paper, in an airtight container in a cool place.

MAKES
16

HANDS-ON
25
MINS

BAKE
50
MINS

Begin the salted caramel for these heavenly brownies at least 2 hours before you intend to bake, so that it has time to cool and firm up.

Chocolate & Salted Caramel Brownies

FOR THE SALTED CARAMEL
160g caster sugar
130ml double cream
2 tsp sea-salt flakes,
    plus extra for sprinkling
40g unsalted butter, diced

FOR THE BROWNIE
350g 70% dark chocolate,
    broken into pieces
175g unsalted butter
4 eggs
260g light muscovado sugar
100g caster sugar
1 tsp vanilla paste
200g plain flour
3 tbsp cocoa powder
a pinch of salt

YOU WILL NEED
23cm square cake tin, greased,
    then lined (base and sides)
    with baking paper

1 For the salted caramel, melt the sugar in a medium pan over a medium heat. Swirl the pan without stirring for 8–10 minutes, until the caramel has turned a dark amber colour.

2 In a separate pan bring the cream to the boil, then immediately remove it from the heat and set aside.

3 Remove the caramel from the heat and carefully add the salt and half the cream. (Take care as the mixture will spit.) Once the mixture has settled, add the remaining cream and the butter, and stir together. Return the pan to the heat and cook for 2 minutes, stirring, until thick and smooth.

4 Pour the salted caramel into a bowl. Leave to cool, then cover with cling film and chill for at least 2 hours, until firm but spoonable. When the caramel is almost ready, start the brownies. Heat the oven to 180°C/160°C fan/350°F/Gas 4.

5 Melt the chocolate and butter together in a bowl set over a pan of simmering water, stirring occasionally for 4–5 minutes, until smooth. Remove from the heat and set aside to cool.

6 Using an electric hand whisk, in a large bowl whisk together the eggs and both sugars until thick and pale. Whisk the cooled chocolate mixture and the vanilla into the egg mixture, then sift in the flour, cocoa powder and salt. Fold together until well mixed.

7 Pour the mixture into the prepared tin and level with the back of a spoon. Spoon the caramel onto the brownie mixture and sprinkle with a little sea salt.

8 Bake for 45–50 minutes, or until a skewer inserted into the centre comes out pasty (but not wet). Allow to cool in the tin completely, then remove from the tin and use a hot knife to cut it into squares.

Start the brown butter at least an hour before you intend to bake this cake. If you have four sandwich tins, you can halve the baking time by making the four sponges in one stage, rather than two.

Chocolate Drip Cake

**FOR THE BROWN
BUTTER SPONGE**
250g unsalted butter, diced
200g light muscovado sugar
4 eggs
200g self-raising flour, sifted
1 tsp baking powder

FOR THE CHOCOLATE SPONGE
200g unsalted butter, softened
200g golden caster sugar
1 tsp vanilla paste
4 eggs
50g cocoa powder
2 tbsp whole milk
180g self-raising flour, sifted

FOR THE BUTTERCREAM
200g 70% dark chocolate
100ml double cream
500g unsalted butter, softened
2 tsp vanilla paste
1kg icing sugar, sifted

FOR THE SHARDS
100g 70% dark chocolate
100g white chocolate
edible gold leaf (optional)

TO DECORATE
200g 70% dark chocolate, melted
strawberries, raspberries or
    cherries (or a mixture)
edible gold spray (optional)

YOU WILL NEED
20cm sandwich tins x 2,
    greased, then lined (base
    and sides) with baking paper
large baking tray, lined
    with baking paper
cocktail stick
medium disposable piping bag

1 Make the brown butter sponges. Melt the butter in a pan over a medium–high heat, reduce the heat and simmer for 8–10 minutes, until the butter starts to brown and smell like popcorn. Leave to cool, then chill for 1–2 hours, until set.

2 Heat the oven to 200°C/180°C fan/400°F/Gas 6. Beat the cooled brown butter and the sugar in a stand mixer fitted with the beater, on medium speed for 2–3 minutes, until creamy.

3 With the mixer on a low speed, add the eggs, one at a time, beating well between each addition. Add the flour and baking powder, until combined. Divide the mixture equally between the tins and bake for 20–25 minutes, until a skewer inserted into the centres comes out clean. Leave to cool in the tins for 5 minutes, then turn out onto a wire rack to cool completely.

4 Make the chocolate sponges. Re-line the tins. Beat the butter, sugar and vanilla together in a stand mixer fitted with the beater, on medium speed for 2–3 minutes, until pale and creamy. With the mixer on a low speed, add the eggs, one at a time, beating well between each addition.

5 Combine the cocoa powder and milk in a small bowl, then add to the batter and beat on medium speed for 30–60 seconds, until combined. With the mixer on a low speed, add the flour, until just combined. Divide the mixture equally between the tins and bake for 20–25 minutes, until a skewer inserted into the centres comes out clean. Leave to cool in the tins for 5 minutes, then turn out onto a wire rack to cool completely.

6 Make the buttercream. Put the chocolate and cream in a bowl set over a pan of simmering water. Stir for 2–3 minutes to a smooth ganache. Remove from the heat and leave to cool.

7 Beat the butter and vanilla in a stand mixer fitted with the beater, on high speed for about 1 minute, until very creamy

Continues overleaf

and smooth. Add the icing sugar, one quarter at a time, beating slowly at first, then increasing the speed for 1 minute.

8 Slowly add the cooled ganache and beat until fluffy. Spoon one third of the buttercream into a separate bowl and set aside.

9 To assemble, level the sponges. Put a dab of buttercream on a cake plate, then top with a brown-butter sponge. Cover with one-fifth of the larger portion of buttercream. Top with a chocolate sponge and spread with a fifth of the buttercream. Repeat for the second brown-butter sponge and a further fifth of the buttercream. Place the final chocolate sponge on top.

10 Spread another one fifth of the buttercream around the side of the cake, and the final fifth evenly over the top. Smooth off any excess to create a crumb coat. Chill for 1 hour.

11 Repeat the buttercream process using two thirds of the reserved buttercream to create a thick, even coating. (Set aside the remaining buttercream for attaching the decorations.) Chill the cake while you make the chocolate shards.

12 Melt the dark and white chocolates in separate bowls set over pans of simmering water. Pour the dark chocolate randomly over the lined baking tray, then pour over the white, filling any gaps. Drag the cocktail stick through to marble.

13 Bang the tray firmly on the work surface to get rid of any air bubbles, then leave to set. Add gold leaf to the chocolate as it sets, if you wish. Once set, use a knife to cut it into shards.

14 Make the decoration. Melt the dark chocolate in a bowl set over a pan of simmering water. Remove from the heat and leave to cool for 2–3 minutes.

15 Pour the chocolate into the piping bag and cut a small, 5mm hole in the end. To pipe the drip, hold the bag at the top of the cake and steadily move around the edge, allowing the drips to trail down the sides, varying your squeeze to achieve different lengths. Pipe chocolate over the top of the cake, and spread it evenly with a palette knife.

16 Use the remaining buttercream to attach the shards, fruit and gold-sprayed cherries, as well as extra pieces of gold leaf, if you wish.

Take your time with this cake, and remember that buttercream is forgiving (you can scrape it off and start again!). Keep the cut-out parts of the cake to eat with ice-cream, or make them into cake pops.

Chocolate Piñata Cake

FOR THE SPONGE
460g dark chocolate chips
625g unsalted butter, softened
830g light muscovado sugar
1 tbsp vanilla paste
12 eggs, beaten
415g plain flour, sifted
about 3 handfuls mixed
   sweets of choice, to fill

FOR THE BUTTERCREAM
900g unsalted butter, softened
1½ tbsp vanilla paste
1.8kg icing sugar, sifted
light blue food-colouring paste
red food-colouring paste

YOU WILL NEED
23cm round, deep cake tins x 3,
   greased, then lined (base and
   sides) with baking paper
13cm-diameter circular
   card template
23cm cake card
3 large piping bags, each fitted
   with a small petal nozzle
cake turntable

1 Heat the oven to 180°C/160°C fan/350°F/Gas 4.

2 Melt the chocolate chips in a bowl set over a pan of simmering water. Remove from the heat, then leave to cool.

3 Meanwhile, beat the butter, sugar and vanilla in a stand mixer fitted with the beater, on medium speed for 2–3 minutes, until pale and creamy.

4 On a low speed, add the eggs, a little at a time, beating well between each addition. Pour in the cooled, melted chocolate and mix together. Add the flour and mix until just combined.

5 Divide the mixture between the prepared tins and bake for 45–55 minutes, until a skewer inserted into the centres comes out a little pasty (but not wet). Cool completely in the tins.

6 Make the buttercream. Beat the butter and vanilla in a stand mixer fitted with the beater, on medium speed for 1 minute, until fluffy. With the mixer on a low speed, add the icing sugar, one third at a time, then increase the speed to medium and beat for 2 minutes, until fluffy. Spoon one quarter of the buttercream into a separate bowl and set aside.

7 To assemble, level the sponges and stack two on top of each other. Place the card template on top of the stack and cut around it to create a hole through the centres of the two cakes to give you two cake rings.

8 Place one of the cake rings on the cake card. Using a palette knife, spread half the reserved buttercream over the sponge ring. Top with the second ring, and spread with the remaining half of the reserved buttercream.

9 Completely fill the cavity with sweets, then place the final sponge on top, levelled-side downwards, to enclose. Use some of the remaining buttercream to create a smooth crumb coat, then chill the cake for 30 minutes.

Continues overleaf

Chocolate **103**

10 Divide the remaining buttercream equally between three bowls. Colour one portion light blue, another portion bright red, and leave the final portion white. Place each buttercream into a piping bag fitted with a petal nozzle.

11 Place the cake on a turntable. For the piñata ruffle, using the blue buttercream, hold the petal nozzle against the bottom of the cake, with the wider, fat point touching the cake and the thin part facing outwards. Using a wiggly, wavy motion, pipe around the cake base. Repeat, moving up the cake, with ruffles of white and red buttercream. Keep going, one colour at a time, all the way to the top of the cake.

12 Once you reach the top of the cake, continue piping ruffles in ever-decreasing, concentric circles, until you get to the middle of the cake.

SERVES

HANDS-ON
1 HOUR

BAKE
30 MINS

16

With three layers and topped with chocolate triangles, this gooey cake is simple to make – but also both delicious and impressive. Scale down the quantities by one third for a two-layered version (leave the baking time the same).

Devil's Food Cake

FOR THE CHOCOLATE FUDGE FROSTING
200ml double cream
350g unsalted butter
450g 54% dark chocolate, finely chopped

FOR THE SPONGE
75g cocoa powder, sifted
150g light brown soft sugar
2 tsp vanilla paste
375ml boiling water
200g unsalted butter
225g caster sugar
3 large eggs, beaten
335g plain flour, sifted
1 tsp baking powder
1 tsp bicarbonate of soda

TO DECORATE
150g 70% dark chocolate
edible gold spray

YOU WILL NEED
20cm loose-bottomed sandwich tins x 3, greased, then base-lined with baking paper
sheet of acetate

1 Make the chocolate-fudge frosting. Pour the cream into a medium pan, add the butter and heat, stirring occasionally, until the butter has melted. Bring the mixture to just below boiling, then remove it from the heat. Add the chocolate and whisk until smooth and glossy. Pour the frosting into a bowl and leave to set at room temperature, whisking occasionally.

2 Heat the oven to 180°C/fan 160°C/350°F/Gas 4. Make the sponge. Whisk the cocoa, brown sugar, vanilla and boiling water together in a bowl to dissolve the sugar. Set aside.

3 Beat the butter and caster sugar in a stand mixer fitted with the beater, on medium speed for 3–5 minutes, until pale and creamy. Add the eggs, a little at a time, mixing well between each addition. Beat in the flour, one third at a time, and add the baking powder and bicarbonate of soda.

4 Fold in the chocolate mixture, then divide equally between the three tins. Bake for 25–30 minutes, until a skewer inserted into the centres comes out clean. Leave to cool in the tins for 5 minutes, then turn out onto wire racks to cool completely.

5 To decorate, melt the chocolate in a bowl set over a pan of simmering water. Remove from the heat. Lay the acetate on a cold work surface and pour over the melted chocolate. Spread the chocolate over the acetate until it starts to change colour and is beginning to set. Use a knife to score triangular shapes into the chocolate. Transfer the acetate onto a baking sheet. Freeze until the chocolate has set hard.

6 Place one sponge on a cake plate and spread with about one quarter of the frosting. Top with another sponge and spread as before. Place the remaining sponge on top, then spread and swirl the top and sides with the remaining frosting.

7 Peel away the acetate and arrange the chocolate triangles on top of the cake. Spray with edible gold spray.

Chocolate **107**

These cousins of the brownies are quick and easy to make – which is good, as they are incredibly moreish and one batch is unlikely to last very long!

White Chocolate & Hazelnut Blondies

140g plain flour, sifted
110g ground hazelnuts
a pinch of sea-salt flakes
1 tsp baking powder
180g unsalted butter, diced
180g golden caster sugar
180g light muscovado sugar
3 eggs, beaten
2 tsp vanilla paste
130g hazelnuts, chopped
160g white chocolate chips
2 tbsp runny honey or
    agave syrup

YOU WILL NEED
22cm square cake tin, greased,
    then lined (base and sides)
    with baking paper

1 Heat the oven to 200°C/180°C fan/400°F/Gas 6.

2 Put the flour, ground hazelnuts, sea salt and baking powder in a large bowl.

3 Melt the butter in a large bowl set over a pan of simmering water. Remove from the heat and stir in the caster sugar and muscovado sugar.

4 Add the eggs, a little at a time, and the vanilla paste, then fold in the flour mixture until fully combined.

5 Gently fold in 100g of the chopped nuts and all the chocolate chips until evenly distributed, then pour the mixture into the prepared tin, giving the tin a gentle shake to disperse the mixture evenly.

6 Bake for 25–30 minutes, until a skewer inserted into the centre comes out pasty (but not wet). Remove from the oven, brush with honey or agave syrup and sprinkle with the reserved chopped hazelnuts while the blondie is still warm.

7 Leave the blondie to cool in the tin for 10 minutes, then remove it carefully and transfer it to a wire rack to cool completely before slicing into squares.

SERVES 16

HANDS-ON 3 HOURS

BAKE 1¼ HOURS

Flora's stunning re-invention of the Black Forest gâteau in Series 6 – left naked on the side to part-reveal the tempting filling – has a magical forest of truffles, chocolate trees and cherry gel.

Flora

Black Forest Gâteau

FOR THE CHOCOLATE SPONGE
100g 70% dark chocolate, chopped
175ml boiling water
4 tbsp cocoa powder
125g unsalted butter, softened
350g caster sugar
2 large eggs, beaten
1 tsp bicarbonate of soda
1 tsp vanilla paste
300g plain flour, sifted
125ml double cream

FOR THE CHERRY SPONGE
225g unsalted butter, softened
225g caster sugar
red food-colouring paste
2 tsp freeze-dried sour cherry powder
4 large eggs, beaten
225g self-raising flour, sifted
2–4 tbsp whole milk

FOR THE CHOCOLATE TRUFFLES
100g 70% dark chocolate, chopped
1 tbsp kirsch
100ml double cream
½ tsp vanilla paste
2 tbsp desiccated coconut
1 tbsp freeze-dried sour cherry powder

Continues overleaf

1 For the chocolate sponge, heat the oven to 180°C/160°C fan/350°F/Gas 4. Mix together the chocolate, boiling water and cocoa in a bowl until melted and smooth. Set aside.

2 Beat together the butter and sugar in a stand mixer fitted with the beater, on medium speed for 5 minutes, until pale and creamy. On a low speed, gradually beat in the eggs, then the bicarbonate of soda, vanilla, flour and cream and finally the chocolate mixture. Divide the mixture equally between the tins and bake for 35–40 minutes, until risen and firm to the touch. Leave to cool in the tins for 10 minutes, then turn out onto a wire rack to cool completely. Wash, grease and line the tins.

3 For the cherry sponge, beat the butter and sugar in a stand mixer fitted with the beater, on medium speed for 5 minutes, until pale and creamy. Add the food colouring and cherry powder to give a deep red, then slowly beat in the eggs with a little flour. Fold in the remaining flour and add the milk. Divide the mixture equally between the tins and bake for 25–30 minutes, until risen and firm. Leave to cool in the tins for 10 minutes, then turn out onto a wire rack to cool completely.

4 For the truffles, place the chocolate in a heatproof bowl with the kirsch. Bring the cream and vanilla to the boil in a heavy-based pan, then pour half the mixture on top of the chocolate and stir. Repeat for the remaining cream mixture.

5 Pour the chocolate mixture into a shallow dish and chill to set. Then, use a spoon to scoop out balls and roll some in the coconut and some in the cherry powder. Store in the fridge.

6 For the cherry gel, place the cherries, lemon juice and sugar in a small pan with 50ml of water. Bring to the boil, remove from the heat and blitz using a hand blender until finely chopped. Then, pour the mixture through a sieve into a clean pan and stir in the agar agar.

Continues overleaf

FOR THE CHERRY GEL
100g cherries, stoned
50ml lemon juice
3 tbsp caster sugar
1g agar agar

FOR THE CHOCOLATE TREES
100g 70% dark chocolate,
    chopped
1 tsp freeze-dried cherry pieces,
    plus extra to decorate

FOR THE CHOCOLATE SAUCE
50g 70% dark chocolate,
    chopped
25g unsalted butter
125ml double cream
1 tbsp caster sugar

FOR THE BUTTERCREAM
125g white chocolate, chopped
180g unsalted butter, softened
400g icing sugar, sifted
1 tsp vanilla paste
3 tbsp whole milk

TO DECORATE
300ml double cream
1 tsp vanilla paste
3 tbsp kirsch
400g cherries, half stoned and
    quartered; half left whole
icing sugar, for dusting

YOU WILL NEED
20cm round, deep cake tins x 2,
    greased, then base-lined
    with baking paper
3cm round cutter
small disposable piping bag
baking sheet lined with
    baking paper
large disposable piping bag

7 Place the pan over a high heat and boil until the agar agar dissolves completely. Pour into a shallow container to about 2cm deep and chill for 1 hour to set. Use the 3cm cutter to create the gel discs for decoration.

8 For the chocolate trees, melt the chocolate in a small bowl set over a pan of simmering water. Beat until smooth, then pour the chocolate into the small piping bag. Snip the end and pipe tree shapes of various sizes onto the lined baking sheet. Sprinkle with dried cherry pieces and chill for at least 15 minutes to set.

9 For the chocolate sauce, melt all the ingredients together in a small pan over a low heat, stir until smooth, then set aside.

10 For the buttercream, melt the white chocolate in a small bowl set over a pan of simmering water. Leave to cool slightly.

11 Beat the butter in a stand mixer fitted with the beater, on high speed until very pale. Add the icing sugar and beat for 5 minutes, until almost white. Add the melted chocolate, and the vanilla and milk and beat until smooth. Spoon into the large piping bag and snip a 2cm hole in the end.

12 In a bowl, whip the double cream and vanilla for the decoration with an electric hand whisk to soft peaks.

13 To assemble, brush all the cake layers with some kirsch. Pipe a little buttercream on a cake plate and top with a chocolate sponge. Pipe large dots of buttercream all the way around the edge of this and the other chocolate layer and on one of the cherry layers. Spread chocolate sauce in the middle of each buttercream ring. Top with quartered cherries, then spread with a little cream until level with the buttercream dots.

14 For the second cherry sponge, pipe a dot of buttercream then drag the piping bag into the centre of the cake to create a droplet shape. Repeat all the way around the cake.

15 Place the first cherry sponge on top of the chocolate sponge on the stand. Add the second chocolate sponge and finish with the cherry layer with the buttercream design. Add the trees on top of the cake, along with some truffles, whole, fresh cherries and the little discs of gel. Dust with icing sugar and extra dried cherry pieces. Serve with the remaining truffles.

Once you've tried these, you'll never go back to shop-bought versions. They need a little skill in the rolling, but are otherwise really easy to make.

Chocolate Mini Rolls

FOR THE SPONGE
60g cocoa powder, sifted
30g unsalted butter, melted
1 tsp vanilla extract
4 tbsp boiling water
150g caster sugar
6 large eggs, separated

FOR THE FILLING
150g unsalted butter, softened
300g icing sugar, sifted
1 tsp peppermint essence

TO DECORATE
200g 70% dark chocolate
200g milk chocolate
100g white chocolate

YOU WILL NEED
30 x 20cm Swiss roll tins x 2,
   greased, then base-lined
   with greased baking paper
2 sheets of baking paper
small disposable piping bag

1 Heat the oven to 180°C/160°C fan/350°F/Gas 4. Make the sponge. Combine the cocoa powder, butter, vanilla and boiling water in a small bowl. Set aside.

2 Whisk together 100g of the sugar and the egg yolks in a separate bowl, until pale, thick and fluffy. Add the chocolate mixture and whisk to combine.

3 In a separate bowl, using an electric hand whisk, whisk the egg whites to stiff peaks. Add the remaining caster sugar and whisk to dissolve. Beat one third of the meringue mixture into the chocolate mixture to loosen. Using a large metal spoon, fold in the remaining meringue mixture until fully combined.

4 Divide the mixture equally between the two prepared tins and level it out. Bake for 12–18 minutes, until springy to the touch. Place the tins on a wire cooling rack, cover the sponges with a damp tea towel and leave to cool completely.

5 Make the filling. With a wooden spoon, beat the butter in a bowl until soft, and gradually add the icing sugar. Add the peppermint essence and beat until white, soft and fluffy.

6 Turn out each sponge onto a sheet of baking paper. Peel off the top layer of baking paper. Turn the sponges so the short ends are facing you. Score a line 4cm in from the nearest short end of each sponge. Spread the filling evenly over each sponge.

7 Take one sponge and, starting from the short edge closest to you, roll it up, stopping in the middle. Repeat from the edge farthest away, until both rolls meet in the middle. Cut down the centre between the rolls.

Continues overleaf

Chocolate **115**

8 Roll and cut the other sponge, so that you have four rolls. Trim the ends and cut each roll into thirds to give 12 mini rolls. Place the rolls, seam-sides down on a cooling rack and chill them for 15 minutes to firm up.

9 To finish, melt the dark and milk chocolates together in a bowl set over a pan of simmering water. Stir to combine.

10 Place the cooling rack with the mini rolls over a baking tin. Spread or pour the chocolate mixture over each mini roll to coat. Leave to set.

11 Melt the white chocolate in a bowl set over a pan of simmering water. Spoon the melted chocolate into the small disposable piping bag and snip a tiny hole the end. Pipe fine stripes across the mini rolls, then leave to set.

John's epic show-stopping creation from Series 3 is altogether divine – with lemon and coconut cakes representing heaven and the deeply indulgent chocolate cake representing hell.

John

Heaven & Hell Cake

FOR THE HELL CAKE
60g cocoa powder
230ml hot water
9 large eggs, separated
155ml sunflower oil
2½ tsp vanilla paste
450g golden caster sugar
1½ tsp bicarbonate of soda
1½ tsp fine salt
finely grated zest of 2 large
   unwaxed oranges
320g plain flour, sifted

FOR THE HEAVEN CAKES
3 large eggs, separated
60ml sunflower oil
90ml chilled water
1 tsp vanilla paste
125g golden caster sugar
finely grated zest of 1 large
   unwaxed lemon
165g plain flour, sifted
½ tsp baking powder
a pinch of salt
150g homemade or good-
   quality lemon curd

**FOR THE HELL GANACHE
& FILLING**
300ml double cream
400g 54% dark chocolate,
   finely chopped
6 tbsp homemade or
   good-quality cherry jam

Continues overleaf

1 Heat the oven to 170°C/150°C fan/325°F/Gas 3. For the hell cake, combine the cocoa powder and hot water until smooth. Set aside to cool a little. Place the egg yolks in a large mixing bowl and, using a wooden spoon, stir in the oil, vanilla, caster sugar, bicarbonate of soda, salt and orange zest. Stir in the cooled cocoa mixture, then add the flour, beating until smooth.

2 Whisk the egg whites in the clean, grease-free bowl of a stand mixer fitted with the whisk, to stiff peaks. Fold the egg whites into the mixture, then spoon into the lined 25cm tin. Level the top and bake for 1 hour 30 minutes, until a skewer inserted into the centre comes out clean. Cool in the tin for 15 minutes, then turn out onto a wire rack to cool completely.

3 For the heaven cakes, place the egg yolks in a large mixing bowl and, using a balloon whisk, mix in the oil, water, vanilla, caster sugar, lemon zest, flour, baking powder and salt.

4 Whisk the egg whites in the clean, grease-free bowl of a stand mixer fitted with the whisk, to stiff peaks. Fold the egg whites into the mixture, then divide it equally between the mini tins. Bake for 15–17 minutes, until pale golden brown and just firm. Leave to cool in the tins for 15 minutes, then turn out onto a wire rack to cool completely. Then, level the tops.

5 Spoon the lemon curd into the piping bag fitted with the jam nozzle and 'inject' each small cake with lemon curd.

6 For the hell ganache, pour the cream into a medium pan over a medium heat and bring just to the boil. Remove from the heat, add the chocolate and leave to stand for 5 minutes, then stir until smooth. Leave to cool until thick, but spreadable.

7 Cut the chocolate cake in half horizontally. Spread the bottom half with the cherry jam and a little of the ganache, then top with the other cake half. Turn the whole cake upside down onto the large cake card.

Continues overleaf

FOR THE HELL MIRROR GLAZE
4 tbsp chilled water
2 platinum-grade
gelatine leaves
200g caster sugar
2 tbsp golden syrup
150g cocoa powder, sifted
120ml double cream

**FOR THE HEAVEN MERINGUE
& FILLING**
2 egg whites
100g caster sugar
¼ tsp cream of tartar
¼ tsp vanilla paste
100g desiccated coconut
5 sheets of edible gold leaf

TO DECORATE THE HELL CAKE
200g 54% dark chocolate

YOU WILL NEED
25cm round, deep cake tin,
greased, then base-lined
with baking paper
5cm round mini-cake tins x 12,
greased
medium piping bag fitted
with a jam nozzle
30cm cake card
2 medium piping bags,
each fitted with a medium
star nozzle
sugar thermometer
6 straws or dowels
15cm cake card
kitchen blowtorch
small piping bag fitted with
a small writing nozzle
sheet of baking paper
2 strips of baking paper,
each measuring 35 x 8cm

8 Spread the top and sides with a thin layer of ganache, then chill for at least 10 minutes, or until set. Repeat with a second, thicker coat of ganache as neatly as possible. Chill again for another 15 minutes, until set. Spoon the remaining ganache into a medium piping bag fitted with a medium star nozzle and chill until thick enough to pipe.

9 For the hell mirror glaze, place the cold water in a shallow bowl, add the gelatine and soak for 5 minutes. Boil the sugar in 100ml of water in a medium pan over a high heat for about 3 minutes, to dissolve. Leave to cool for 1 minute then, using a balloon whisk, stir in the golden syrup and cocoa until smooth. Squeeze out the gelatine and add it to the glaze, followed by the cream. Whisk until smooth. Place the chilled cake on a wire rack set over a tray to catch the drips, and pour the glaze over the cake. Spread gently over the sides to cover.

10 For the heaven meringue, place the egg whites, sugar and cream of tartar in a bowl set over a pan of simmering water. Whisk for 3–4 minutes, until it reaches 48°C/118°F on a sugar thermometer. Remove from the pan and whisk until the mixture cools and forms stiff, shiny peaks. Whisk in the vanilla.

11 Cover the top and sides of each mini cake with meringue and roll in coconut. Stack the cakes on the small cake card in a circle, seven cakes on the base, then four and then one on top, using straws or dowelling to hold them in place. Place the remaining meringue in the remaining medium piping bag fitted with a medium star nozzle.

12 Place the small card on top of the chocolate cake and pipe swirls of meringue around the base of the board to cover it. Brown the piped meringue with a blowtorch until just golden. Decorate the heaven cakes with flakes of gold leaf.

13 To decorate the hell cake, temper the chocolate (see page 93), place a little into the small piping bag with the writing nozzle and pipe 'Tartarus' (the pit beneath Hades!) onto a sheet of baking paper. Leave to set. Spread the remaining chocolate thinly onto the strips of baking paper. Cool until set, then break into shards and arrange around the cake. Place the 'Tartarus' on top of the cake, then pipe the remaining ganache around the base.

The piping on this cake looks impressive, but is actually easy to master – just keep your hand steady and take your time.

White Chocolate & Blueberry Cake

FOR THE SPONGE
200g unsalted butter, softened
200g golden caster sugar
1 tsp vanilla paste
4 eggs
200g self-raising flour, sifted
200g blueberries
100g white chocolate shavings,
   to decorate

FOR THE BUTTERCREAM
300g white chocolate chips
115g double cream
450g unsalted butter, softened
900g icing sugar, sifted
75g homemade or good-quality
   blueberry jam

YOU WILL NEED
20cm sandwich tins x 3,
   greased, then lined (base
   and sides) with baking paper
large piping bag, fitted with
   a large closed star nozzle

1 Preheat the oven to 200°C/180°C fan/400°F/Gas 6.

2 Beat the butter, sugar and vanilla in a stand mixer fitted with the beater on medium speed for 2–3 minutes, until the mixture is pale and creamy. With the mixer on low, add the eggs one at a time, beating well. Then gently mix in the flour, until just combined.

3 Using a spatula, gently fold in the blueberries, then divide the mixture equally between the tins. Bake the sponges for 20–25 minutes, until golden brown and a skewer inserted into the centres comes out clean. Leave to cool in the tins.

4 Make the buttercream. Melt the white chocolate chips and cream in a bowl set over a pan of simmering water, stirring occasionally. Remove from the heat and set aside to cool.

5 Beat the butter and icing sugar in a stand mixer fitted with the beater, on medium speed for 1–2 minutes, until fluffy. Reduce the speed to low and add the cooled, melted chocolate, mixing for 20–30 seconds, until fully combined. Reserve one third of the buttercream in a separate bowl.

6 To assemble, place one of the sponges, top-side down, on a cake plate. Spread over one quarter of the buttercream from the mixer bowl. Top with a second sponge, and spread with another quarter. Top with the remaining sponge, then use a further quarter of the buttercream to create a crumb coat over the sides and top of the cake. Chill the cake for 30 minutes.

7 Use the final quarter of the buttercream to cover the side of the cake. Press the chocolate shavings around the side to cover.

8 Lightly stir the blueberry jam through the reserved buttercream to create a ripple effect. Spoon this into the piping bag fitted with the star nozzle. Beginning around the outside edge and working inwards, pipe spirals of ripple icing to look like roses all over the top of the cake.

You'll need only a tiny slice of Mary-Anne's cake-come-dessert (from Series 2) to feel satisfied. It's a brilliant option if you're feeding a crowd.

Chocolate & Orange Mousse Cake

Mary-Anne

FOR THE JOCONDE PASTE
100g unsalted butter, softened
100g icing sugar, sifted
100g pasteurised egg whites
110g plain flour, sifted
orange food-colouring gel

FOR THE JOCONDE
225g ground almonds
225g icing sugar, sifted
6 eggs
40g plain flour, sifted
40g cocoa powder
180g pasteurised egg whites
25g granulated sugar
85g clarified butter, melted

FOR THE MOUSSE
juice and finely grated zest
   of 1 unwaxed orange
1 tsp powdered gelatine
300ml double cream
175g 54% dark chocolate,
   broken into pieces
2 eggs, separated

FOR THE GELÉE
1 tbsp arrowroot powder
150ml smooth orange juice

TO DECORATE
pared zest of 1 unwaxed orange,
   cut into thin strips
150ml double cream

Continues overleaf

1 Heat the oven to 220°C/200°C fan/425°F/Gas 7.

2 For the joconde paste, beat the butter and icing sugar in a stand mixer fitted with the beater, on medium speed for 3 minutes, until fluffy. Gradually add the egg whites, beating continuously, until fully combined.

3 Fold in the flour, then mix in enough food colouring to give the desired orange shade. Spoon the mixture into the large piping bag fitted with the plain nozzle. Pipe the mixture onto the baking trays in random swirls and chill for 10 minutes.

4 For the joconde, beat the almonds, icing sugar and eggs together in a stand mixer fitted with the beater, on medium speed for 5 minutes, until light and fluffy. Add the flour and cocoa powder and mix until combined.

5 Place the egg whites in a large, clean, grease-free bowl and, using an electric hand whisk, whisk to soft peaks. Add the granulated sugar and continue whisking to stiff peaks. Using a metal spoon, gently fold the meringue mixture into the chocolate mixture. Mix a large spoonful of the sponge batter into the clarified butter, then fold this back into the sponge.

6 Remove the piped joconde paste from the fridge. Divide the sponge mixture equally between the two trays, smoothing it level over the paste. Bake for 7–8 minutes, until the sponges are lightly browned. Cover each sponge with a sheet of baking paper, then invert the baking trays onto the work surface and peel off the paper to reveal the pattern. Leave to cool.

7 Using the springform tin as a guide, cut out two circles of sponge to fit inside. Place one circle in the base of the tin. Cut long strips of sponge about 5cm wide and use these to

Continues overleaf

YOU WILL NEED
large piping bag fitted
  with a 5mm plain nozzle
45 x 30cm baking trays x 2,
  lined with baking paper,
  then brushed with
  melted butter
2 sheets of baking paper
25cm springform tin,
  greased, then base-lined
  with baking paper
skewers or chopsticks
large piping bag fitted with
  a large closed star nozzle

line the sides of the tin, ensuring the pattern is facing outwards, and there are no gaps. Set aside.

8 For the mousse, pour the orange juice into a small bowl and sprinkle over the gelatine. Set the mixture aside for 3 minutes, then set the bowl over a small pan of simmering water and stir gently to dissolve the gelatine. Whisk the cream to soft peaks.

9 Place the chocolate in a bowl set over a pan of gently simmering water, and stir gently until melted. Remove the bowl from the heat, then stir in the orange zest, egg yolks and gelatine until well combined. Fold in the whisked cream.

10 Place the egg whites in a clean, grease-free bowl and, using an electric hand whisk, whisk to stiff (but not dry) peaks. Gently fold the egg whites into the chocolate mixture until well combined.

11 Pour the mousse into the sponge-lined tin and place the remaining circle of sponge on top. Press down to ensure it's flat. If necessary, trim the sponge around the side of the cake so that it's level with the top. Chill for at least 2 hours.

12 For the gelée, mix the arrowroot powder with 1 tablespoon of orange juice, then stir it into the rest of the juice. Transfer the mixture to a pan and heat gently until it thickens and clears (about 4–5 minutes). Set aside to cool.

13 Carefully remove the cake from the tin and place it on a serving plate or cake stand. To make the orange curls for the decoration, wind the thin strips of orange zest around the skewers or chopsticks, then set aside. Pour the cooled gelée over the mousse cake, and return the cake to the fridge for 30 minutes to set.

14 Using an electric hand whisk, whisk the cream for the decoration to soft peaks and spoon it into the piping bag fitted with the star nozzle. Once the cake has set, pipe the cream around the top edge, then decorate with the orange curls.

Miranda's meringue cake from Series 1 is a hybrid celebration of the best of sweet baking: chocolate brownie, fluffy meringue, and lashings of berries and cream.

Miranda

Brownie Meringue Cake

FOR THE BROWNIE
200g 70% dark chocolate, roughly chopped
200g unsalted butter, softened
250g icing sugar, sifted
3 eggs, beaten
110g plain flour, sifted

FOR THE MERINGUE TOPPING
4 egg whites
¼ tsp cream of tartar
200g caster sugar
100g roasted hazelnuts, chopped

FOR THE FILLING
300ml whipping cream, well chilled
100g icing sugar, sifted
300g raspberries

TO DECORATE
200g raspberries
100g roasted hazelnuts, roughly chopped
100g pistachios, roughly chopped

YOU WILL NEED
20cm sandwich tins x 2, greased, then base-lined with baking paper

1 Heat the oven to 190°C/170°C fan/ 375°F/Gas 5. For the brownie base, place 180g of the chocolate in a bowl set over a pan of steaming water. Allow to melt, stirring frequently, until smooth. Remove from the heat and set aside to cool.

2 Beat the butter and icing sugar in a stand mixer fitted with the beater, until pale and fluffy. Gradually add the eggs, a little at the time, then beat in the flour, one third at a time, until the mixture is smooth. Beat in the cooled, melted chocolate.

3 Fold in the remaining 20g of chopped chocolate. Divide the mixture between the tins and level with a palette knife. Bake for 8 minutes, until the mixture has started to form a crust.

4 While the mixture is baking, start the meringue topping. Pour the egg whites and cream of tartar into a stand mixer fitted with the whisk. Whisk to stiff peaks, then whisk in the sugar, one quarter at a time, to a smooth, glossy meringue. With the mixer on low, whisk in the hazelnuts.

5 Take the cake tins out of the oven and reduce the temperature to 170°C/150°C fan/325°F/Gas 3. Divide the meringue between the two tins, covering the brownie. Smooth the surface of one of the meringues and 'peak' the surface of the other. Bake for a further 25 minutes, until the meringue is firm. Remove from the oven and leave to cool in the tins.

6 For the filling, using an electric hand whisk, whisk the cream to soft peaks, then add the icing sugar and two thirds of the raspberries. Whisk briefly to a thick, pink cream. Gently fold in the remaining raspberries.

7 Loosen the brownies with a round-bladed knife. Turn out the brownie with the flat-topped meringue onto a plate, meringue-side downwards. Spread with the raspberry cream, then top with the second brownie, peaked meringue upwards. Decorate with the raspberries, hazelnuts and pistachios before serving.

Rahul's moist chocolate cake from Series 9 is surrounded by crunchy chocolate soil and decorated with a piped garden. Feel free to be creative with your garden design, if you like.

Rahul

Edible Rock Garden Cake

FOR THE SPONGE
100g cocoa powder, sifted
120ml boiling water
600g dark brown soft sugar
200g baking margarine or
    softened unsalted butter
6 eggs
350g self-raising flour, sifted
2 tsp baking powder

**FOR THE ITALIAN
MERINGUE BUTTERCREAM**
200g caster sugar
4 egg whites
250g salted butter, diced
250g unsalted butter, diced
1 tsp orange extract
1 tsp vanilla extract
1 tsp lemon extract
green food-colouring gel
    or paste
red food-colouring gel or paste

FOR THE CHOCOLATE SOIL
100g caster sugar
75g 70% dark chocolate,
    roughly chopped

YOU WILL NEED
20cm sandwich tins x 2,
    greased and base-lined
    with baking paper
15cm round cake tins x 2,
    greased and base-lined
    with baking paper
sugar thermometer
plate lined with baking paper
2 small disposable piping bags

1 Heat the oven to 180°C/160°C fan/350°F/Gas 4.

2 Beat the cocoa and boiling water in a stand mixer fitted with the beater, on medium speed to combine, then add the remaining sponge ingredients and mix until everything is fully incorporated.

3 Divide the mixture proportionately between the four prepared tins. Bake for 25–30 minutes, or until a skewer inserted into the centres comes out clean. Cool in the tins for 5 minutes, then turn out onto a wire rack to cool completely.

4 Make the Italian meringue buttercream. Heat the caster sugar and 100ml of water in a medium pan over a medium heat to dissolve the sugar, then increase the heat and boil until the syrup reaches about 110°C/230°F on a sugar thermometer.

5 Leave the syrup on the heat and whisk the egg whites in the clean, grease-free bowl of a stand mixer to soft peaks. Keep the whisk running and, when the sugar syrup has reached 121°C/250°F, remove the pan from heat and slowly pour the syrup in a thin, steady stream into the egg whites. Whisk until the outside of the bowl is at room temperature and the meringue is very thick and glossy.

6 Then, start adding cubes of salted and unsalted butter, whisking after each addition to make a smooth, thick buttercream. Add the orange, vanilla and lemon extracts and mix thoroughly. Cover, and chill until firm.

7 Make chocolate soil. Heat 2 tablespoons of water and the sugar in a small pan over a medium heat until the sugar dissolves. Increase the heat and boil the mixture until it turns golden around the edges (or reaches 135°C/275°F on a sugar thermometer). Stir in the chopped chocolate – it will immediately form clumps and crumbs. Tip this onto the lined plate and leave to cool.

Continues overleaf

Chocolate **131**

8 To assemble, sandwich the two larger cakes with 3 tablespoons of the buttercream, spread evenly. Spread 1 tablespoon of buttercream on top.

9 Sandwich the two smaller cakes with about 2 tablespoons of buttercream and stack these on top of the larger cakes.

10 Place 6 tablespoons of buttercream in a small bowl and add green food colouring to make a leaf colour. Place 4 tablespoons of plain buttercream in a second bowl and colour this red.

11 Spread the remaining plain buttercream around the top and sides of the stacked cake.

12 Place the red and green buttercreams in separate, small disposable piping bags. Snip off the tip of the bag of red icing and make a v-shaped cut in the end of the bag of green icing.

13 Pipe green leaves around the sides of both cake layers and a few on the top, adding red dots to make flowers. Sprinkle the soil around the bottom of each cake layer and sprinkle a little on top. Chill the cake and serve within 2 days.

Rob's gâteau (Series 2), layered with rich mousse, could easily double up as a dessert. Use mini balloons to make the chocolate bowls.

Rob

Raspberry Chocolate Cake

FOR THE CHOCOLATE SPONGE
4 eggs
125g caster sugar
a pinch of salt
55g unsalted butter, melted
110g plain flour
1 tbsp cocoa powder

FOR THE PLAIN SPONGE
4 eggs
125g caster sugar
a pinch of salt
55g unsalted butter, melted
125g plain flour

FOR THE MOUSSE
220g 54% dark chocolate
80g unsalted butter
6 egg yolks
200g caster sugar
4 egg whites
200ml double cream

FOR THE GANACHE
200ml double cream
50g light muscovado sugar
200g 70% dark chocolate,
   broken into pieces

FOR THE CHOCOLATE RECTANGLES
200g 70% dark chocolate
200g white chocolate

FOR THE CHOCOLATE BOWLS
200g 70% dark chocolate
200g raspberries
dark and white chocolate
   cigars, to decorate

Continues overleaf

1 Heat the oven to 180°C/160°C fan/350°F/Gas 4. Place the eggs, sugar and salt in a bowl set over a pan of barely simmering water. Using an electric hand whisk, whisk on high speed until the mixture is thick and mousse-like, and leaves a ribbon trail when you lift the whisk.

2 Remove the bowl from the heat and whisk for 2–3 minutes to cool the mixture slightly. Drizzle half the melted butter around the side of the mixture and sift over half the flour. Fold in with a large metal spoon, then drizzle in the remaining butter and sift over the remaining flour and the cocoa. Fold very gently until mixed. Carefully pour the mixture into the lined cake tin.

3 Repeat the method in steps 1 and 2 for the plain sponge (this time sifting in only flour and no cocoa powder).

4 Bake both sponges for 30–35 minutes, until firm and slightly shrinking away from the sides. Leave to cool in the tins for 5 minutes, then turn out onto a wire rack to cool completely.

5 For the mousse, melt the chocolate and butter together in a bowl set over a pan of simmering water. Remove the bowl from the heat and set aside. Whisk the egg yolks in the bowl of a stand mixer fitted with the whisk until pale and creamy.

6 Dissolve the sugar with 150ml of water in a small pan over a low heat, swirling the pan occasionally, until boiling. Boil until the temperature reaches 120°C/248°F on a sugar thermometer. Very slowly pour the syrup in a thin stream into the egg yolks, whisking continuously on a high speed until the mixture leaves a ribbon trail when you lift the whisk.

7 In a clean, grease-free bowl, whisk the egg whites to soft peaks. In a separate bowl, whisk the double cream to soft peaks. Gently fold the chocolate mixture into the egg and sugar mixture, then fold in the whisked cream, then the egg whites, until everything is fully combined. Chill until needed.

Continues overleaf

YOU WILL NEED
23cm springform tins x 2,
    greased, then base-lined
    with baking paper
    and dusted
sugar thermometer
extra sheets of baking paper
3 mini balloons

8 Cut each cooled cake in half horizontally. Wash one of the cake tins and re-line with baking paper that comes 5cm above the side of the tin. Place one plain sponge in the base of the tin, top with one third of the mousse, then place a chocolate sponge on top. Follow with another third of the mousse, then another plain sponge, the remaining chocolate mouse and finish with the chocolate sponge. Chill for about 1 hour, to set.

9 For the ganache, heat the double cream with the muscovado sugar in a medium pan until the sugar has dissolved (about 3–5 minutes). Boil for 1 minute, then leave to cool for 1 minute. Add the chocolate, leave for 5 minutes, then stir until smooth.

10 Remove the cake from the fridge and pour half the ganache over the top, then return the cake to the fridge until the ganache has set (at least 5 minutes). Remove the cake from the tin, peel away the paper and place on a cake plate or stand. Spread the sides of the cake with the remaining ganache.

11 For the chocolate rectangles, melt the dark and white chocolates in separate bowls set over pans of simmering water. On sheets of baking paper, spread out the melted chocolate into two (one dark and one white) rectangles measuring about 35 x 15cm. Chill for at least 15 minutes, to set.

12 Using a hot knife, cut the set chocolate into rectangles, each measuring about 10 x 2cm. Place the chocolate rectangles around the side of the cake, alternating in colour.

13 For the chocolate bowls, blow up the three small balloons to about 10cm diameter and tie a knot in the top. Line a baking tray with baking paper. Melt the chocolate in a small bowl set over a pan of simmering water.

14 When the chocolate has melted, dip the balloons in, holding them by the knotted end so that the chocolate comes one third of the way up the inflated parts. Place the balloons onto the lined tray, holding them for a few seconds so the chocolate pools around the base of the balloon a little to support them. Chill for 1–2 hours, until set, then snip the balloons and carefully peel the rubber away from the chocolate.

15 Fill the chocolate bowls with raspberries and place them on top of the cake. Decorate with chocolate cigars.

CHAPTER THREE

Bakers' Favourites

MEET THE BAKERS

HENRY, 20, DURHAM
ENGLISH STUDENT

Henry's love of baking was inspired by *Bake Off* – as a child he would walk past the tent every day on his way to and from school. Henry grew up in Ilford and is currently studying English Literature at university. His housemates think he's completely bonkers when he's frequently up baking until 2am in an attempt to perfect an undoubtedly difficult bake. He's involved in a large number of clubs and societies at university, and both acts and plays music at university events, but he can always find time to whip up a showstopper.

JAMIE, 20, SURREY
PART-TIME WAITER

Jamie's grandma and parents taught him the baking basics, but it was after an episode of *Bake Off* inspired him to make a plaited loaf that his baking aspirations really took hold. Born and raised in Surrey, Jamie is working as a part-time waiter in the lead-up to studying Sports Science at university. He happily takes on more technically difficult bakes, such as a croquembouche and croissants and has a fairly traditional approach to his flavours – although he likes to experiment with what he can find in the house.

ALICE, 28, LONDON
GEOGRAPHY TEACHER

Alice grew up in a seaside town in Essex. At 15 years old, while recovering from a back operation for scoliosis and no longer able to do sport, she turned her hand to baking – and perfected the fruit pavlova while she was living in New Zealand in her early 20s. After returning to the UK, she trained to be a Geography teacher. Now living in east London, she uses cakes in her lessons – demonstrating everything from coastal erosion to volcanic activity. She loves making highly decorative layered cakes, and puff pastry. Her baking style is intricate and delicate, full of flavour and enthusiasm – and has to make people go 'wow!'

MICHAEL, 24,
STRATFORD-UPON-AVON
THEATRE MANAGER/FITNESS
INSTRUCTOR

Michael's mother taught him to bake, encouraging him to learn from old, handwritten recipes passed down from his mother's grandparents. He was born in Newcastle, but considers himself Scottish as he moved to Scone in Scotland at age seven and studied in Edinburgh. In his baking, though, he is especially inspired by the flavours of his Indian heritage. He now works as a manager at a theatre company in Stratford-upon-Avon. Michael has attempted pretty much every discipline in baking, but his strengths lie in cakes and pastry.

PHIL, 56, ESSEX
HGV DRIVER

Phil was introduced to the joys of baking bread in his home economics class at school, but it wasn't until six years ago that he started to take baking seriously. He now bakes four or five times a week, frequently making focaccia, granary bread and brioche, but also pastry (he likes the challenge of hot-water crust, puff and choux). Phil grew up in Barking, training to be a driver at age 17. He now lives in Rainham, with his wife and two daughters. Working the early shifts means that Phil can spend the rest of his day preparing some of the meals and baking treats for his family and friends. He is passionate about motorbikes and always turns up for biking meetings with bakes. He has been working really hard on his decoration and piping techniques over the last year and now also loves to create really delicately decorated cakes.

AMELIA, 24, HALIFAX
FASHION DESIGNER

Amelia has been baking for 19 years – watching her mum and grandma creating beautiful cake decorations inspired her to start baking as a child. Born to a Caribbean father and British/half-Polish mother, Amelia grew up in Halifax and studied in Leeds and Leicester. She honed her baking skills while at university, baking for friends and college fundraising events. Now living in London and working as a sportswear designer, Amelia draws on her northern roots to inspire her baking and believes that freshly farmed produce is essential for a satisfying bake. One of her proudest bakes is a snow leopard cake that she baked for her nephew's fifth birthday – a Madeira and a chocolate sponge with intricately designed tiger and snow-leopard faces.

DAN, 32, ROTHERHAM
SUPPORT WORKER

Dan is predominantly a self-taught baker, but has fond memories of his mum showing him how to bake a Victoria sponge as a child and his army chef dad coming to school to teach how to plait and bake bread. He got serious about baking at age 21 in a bid to impress his then girlfriend (now wife) with a themed birthday cake. Born in Worksop and raised in Rotherham, Dan lives just 20 minutes away from where he grew up, with wife Laura and their three dogs. Dan's favourite part of the baking process is decoration and he loves producing awe-inspiring bakes. He made his own wedding cake and says the thing he is most proud of making is a towering croquembouche.

DAVID, 36, LONDON
INTERNATIONAL
HEALTH ADVISER

David grew up in rural Yorkshire, where his mum (who baked all the time – the family never ate a shop-bought loaf at home) inspired him to start baking. His passion was further developed by his travels to Malawi (among other places), where he learnt to build an oven out of an oil drum and invented a cake that could steam-cook over a village fire. David studied art and design before switching to nursing. When he's not travelling the world for work, he lives in London and has lots of hobbies like cycling and ceramics. David's baking repertoire is broad, but his strengths lie in bread. He's not into fancy, colourful icings, but prefers robust flavours and good, solid bakes.

HELENA, 40, LEEDS
ONLINE PROJECT MANAGER

Helena spent much of her childhood watching her Spanish grandmother cook and bake, but it was only after moving to Las Vegas as part of an exchange scheme at school and living with a Mormon family that Helena really started baking. She was born in Ceuta (an independent Spanish city in north Africa), raised in Lanzarote and studied in mainland Spain. During her degree, she moved to Leeds on an exchange, and then married her one-time lodger. They have a daughter. Helena likes to use American flavours, such as pumpkin, pecans, maple and cinnamon in her bakes. She also likes to use traditional Spanish flavours, including almond and paprika, as well as incorporating her passion for all things Halloween into her baking creations.

PRIYA, 34, LEICESTER MARKETING CONSULTANT

Priya's first foray into baking was at an after-school baking club at primary school. Then, seven years ago, when she was given a stand mixer as a wedding gift, she went 'baking bonkers'. She now bakes with such enthusiasm that she's been known to bake bread well into the night. A freelance marketing consultant and self-styled perfectionist, Priya lives in Leicester with her husband and two children, and is writing her first novel. She's recently experimented with vegan baking and loves tropical, fruity flavours. She'd love to travel on a worldwide sweet-and-savoury tasting tour.

MICHELLE, 35, WALES PRINT SHOP ADMINISTRATOR

Michelle first fell in love with baking as a child watching her mother doing traditional baking at home. She grew up on a farm and now lives in the seaside town of Tenby with her husband and teenage son. Michelle bakes almost every other day – whether that's making a simple loaf to have for breakfast or something sweet to eat for dessert. She loves experimenting with flavour combinations and using seasonal vegetables from her own vegetable patch. Her bakes are precise and finessed, and created with an emphasis on good-quality, local produce.

ROSIE, 28, SOMERSET VETERINARY SURGEON

Rosie's baking passions began aged five, when she was given a children's baking book. She grew up in Oxfordshire, studied at Cambridge, and now lives in Somerset with her childhood-sweetheart husband and many animals. When Rosie's not treating drunken hedgehogs, performing spleen surgery on dogs, or on call, she'll be baking to unwind and keep the practice nurses well-fed. With a love of patisserie, a little box of mixed pastries is Rosie's 'go-to' bake. Her baking is inspired by her rural surroundings, from the orchards next door, to the fresh eggs laid by her ducks and chickens.

STEPH, 28, CHESTER SHOP ASSISTANT

Steph's grandad got her baking, with his love of homemade bread. She has been baking with a vengeance for the past three or so years. She is primarily self-taught and considers herself an 'intermediate, still-learning' baker. Steph's passion for sport and wellness inspires her baking: she enjoys the challenge of making her bakes healthier in whatever ways she can – adding vegetables or fruit, lowering the refined sugar and prioritising more nutritious fats. Biscuits are Steph's 'go-to' bake, but her signature bake is a sourdough loaf using her starter, which she calls 'Sammy'.

SERVES
12

HANDS-ON
25
MINS

BAKE
45
MINS

Phil

Inspired by his wife's lemon drizzle, Phil road-tested his lime cake first at a bike-club quiz night. Over time, he has customised it further – baking it in a bundt tin and adding the lime crunch.

Lime & Coconut Bundt Drizzle

FOR THE SPONGE
230g unsalted butter, softened
230g caster sugar
4 eggs, beaten
230g self-raising flour, sifted
65g desiccated coconut
juice and finely grated zest
   of 1 unwaxed lime

FOR THE LIME CRUNCH
finely grated zest of
   2 unwaxed limes
2 tsp caster sugar

FOR THE DRIZZLE
3 tbsp lime juice
3 tbsp icing sugar, sifted

FOR THE ICING
100g icing sugar, sifted
1 tbsp lime juice

YOU WILL NEED
1.5-litre bundt tin, well greased
sheet of baking paper
small disposable piping bag

1 Heat the oven to 180°C/160°C fan/350°F/Gas 4.

2 Beat the butter and sugar in a stand mixer fitted with the beater, on medium speed for 5–6 minutes, until pale and creamy. With the mixer on a low speed, add the eggs, a little at a time, beating well between each addition.

3 Using a large metal spoon, fold in the flour, coconut, and lime juice and zest until just combined.

4 Spoon the mixture into the prepared tin and level the surface. Bake for 40–45 minutes, until golden brown and a skewer inserted into the ring comes out clean.

5 While the cake is baking, make the lime crunch. Mix together the zest and caster sugar in a bowl, then transfer the mixture to a piece of baking paper and set it aside to dry slightly.

6 Make the drizzle. Use a wooden spoon to combine the lime juice and icing sugar in a small bowl, until smooth.

7 When the cake is ready, remove it from the oven, prick it all over with a skewer and spoon half the drizzle mixture over the top. Allow the cake to cool for 10 minutes in the tin, then turn it out onto a wire rack. Drizzle over the remaining lime and sugar mixture. Leave to cool completely.

8 Once the cake has cooled, make the icing. Place the icing sugar in a bowl and add enough of the lime juice to make a thick, pourable icing. Spoon the icing into the piping bag, snip off the end and drizzle the icing over the cake, allowing it to collect in the ridges of the bundt.

9 Leave the icing to set slightly before sprinkling the cake with the lime crunch to finish.

This spiced cake is inspired by the golden streusel cake served at breakfast during Henry's childhood family holidays to Germany. You could replace the walnuts with toasted pecans, if you prefer.

Henry

Apple, Maple & Walnut Streusel Cake

FOR THE SPONGE
250g self-raising flour, sifted
½ tsp baking powder
1 tbsp ground cinnamon
½ tsp ground cardamom
½ tsp ground ginger
130g cold unsalted butter, diced
130g light muscovado sugar
250g Bramley apple, peeled, cored
   and chopped into small cubes
110g dried blueberries or sultanas
3 eggs
60g double cream
seeds from 1 vanilla pod

FOR THE STREUSEL TOPPING
35g plain flour
90g demerara sugar
½ tsp ground cinnamon
60g cold unsalted butter, diced
150g walnuts, roughly chopped,
   plus 50g left whole, to decorate

FOR THE MAPLE ICING
50g unsalted butter, softened
60g light muscovado sugar
1 tsp maple syrup
100g full-fat cream cheese

TO SERVE
250g crème fraîche
60g runny honey
1 tsp cinnamon
½ tsp vanilla paste

YOU WILL NEED
20cm deep, loose-bottomed
   or springform cake tin,
   greased, then base-lined
small piping bag fitted with
   a medium closed star nozzle

1 Preheat the oven to 180°C/160°C fan/350°F/Gas 4.

2 Place the flour, baking powder and spices in a large mixing bowl. Rub in the butter, using your fingertips, to a breadcrumb consistency. Stir in the sugar, apple and blueberries or sultanas until evenly distributed.

3 Using a balloon whisk, in a small bowl lightly whisk together the eggs, double cream and vanilla seeds, then stir into the sponge mixture until combined. Spoon the mixture into the prepared tin and level with the back of the spoon. Set aside.

4 For the streusel topping, place the flour, sugar and cinnamon in a mixing bowl. Rub in the butter, using your fingertips, to a breadcrumb consistency. Stir through the chopped walnuts until evenly distributed. Sprinkle the topping over the cake, making sure it is fairly level.

5 Bake the cake for 1 hour 10 minutes, until golden brown on top and a skewer inserted into the centre comes out clean. Carefully loosen the edges of the cake, cool in the tin for 20 minutes, then transfer to a wire rack to cool completely.

6 For the maple icing, beat the butter, sugar and maple syrup together, until fluffy, then beat in the cream cheese until smooth. Place the icing in the small piping bag fitted with the star nozzle and pipe rosettes around the top edge of the cake, placing a whole walnut on top of each to finish.

7 Just before serving, in a small bowl, mix together the crème fraîche, honey, cinnamon and vanilla until well combined. Serve the cake in slices, with the flavoured crème fraîche alongside.

Dan's version of his mum's coffee cake is layered and topped with coffee-flavoured cream cheese buttercream to balance out any bitterness, and then sprinkled with a sweet espresso brittle.

Dan

Layered Coffee Cake

FOR THE SPONGE
2 tbsp espresso instant
    coffee powder
1 tbsp boiling water
340g unsalted butter, softened
340g golden caster sugar
6 large eggs, beaten
1 tbsp golden syrup
340g self-raising flour
1 tsp baking powder

FOR THE ESPRESSO BRITTLE
1 tsp espresso roasted
    coffee beans or instant
    coffee granules
60g unsalted butter, softened
25g liquid glucose
4 tsp whole milk
75g golden icing sugar, sifted

**FOR THE COFFEE & CREAM
CHEESE BUTTERCREAM**
1 tbsp instant espresso coffee
1 tsp boiling water
200g unsalted butter, softened
180g full-fat cream cheese
500g golden icing sugar, sifted

YOU WILL NEED
20cm round, deep cake tins
    or springform tins x 2,
    greased, then base-lined
    with baking paper
33 x 23cm baking tray, lined
    (base and sides) with
    baking paper

1 Preheat the oven to 180°C/160°C fan/350°F/Gas 4. Dissolve the coffee in the boiling water and leave to cool.

2 Beat the butter and sugar in a stand mixer fitted with the beater, on medium speed for about 5 minutes, until light and creamy. With the mixer on a low speed, gradually add the eggs, beating well between each addition. Add the golden syrup and prepared coffee and beat until combined.

3 Sift the flour and baking powder into the creamed mixture, and use a metal spoon to fold gently until incorporated.

4 Divide the mixture between the two prepared tins and bake for 30–35 minutes, until risen and a skewer inserted into the centres comes out clean. Cool in the tins for 5 minutes, then turn out onto a wire rack to cool completely. (Leave the oven on for the brittle.)

5 To make the brittle, place the coffee beans in a resealable sandwich bag or sheet of folded baking paper. Roll over them with a rolling pin to crush. Set aside.

6 Place the butter, glucose and milk in a small pan over a low heat and warm gently for about 1–2 minutes, just until the butter has melted. Add the icing sugar and stir until dissolved.

7 Increase the heat and boil, stirring, for about 4 minutes, until the mixture has reduced by about one third and is syrup-like and thick enough to coat the back of the spoon (it will look thick and frothy).

8 Remove the syrup from the heat and allow it to settle to look like a thick custard. Then, add the crushed coffee beans or instant granules and stir until evenly distributed. Pour the mixture onto the lined baking tray and spread it out quickly and evenly so that it reaches the edges of the tray.

Continues overleaf

9 Bake the brittle for 12–15 minutes, until golden and caramel-like. It will look bubbly, but it will settle once it's out of the oven. Transfer the tray to a wire rack for the brittle to set.

10 To make the buttercream, dissolve the coffee in the boiling water and leave to cool.

11 Put the butter and cream cheese in a mixing bowl and beat with an electric hand whisk until smooth and combined. Gradually add the icing sugar, a few tablespoons at a time, and beat with a wooden spoon for 2–3 minutes, until fluffy. Add the coffee and beat until combined.

12 Cut each cooled cake in half horizontally. Sandwich each cut cake with a generous amount of buttercream. Cover the top of one cake with another layer of buttercream, making sure you leave enough for a generous topping, then stack the other cake on top, giving you a four-tiered cake.

13 Top the cake with the remaining buttercream. Crush the brittle and sprinkle it over the top of the cake, to decorate. (You'll have more brittle than you need – try sprinkling it over your morning porridge, or over vanilla ice cream for a crunchy alternative to an affogato.)

This is Rosie's mum's chocolate beetroot cake. She makes it for all family birthdays, every year. It's a super-moist, super-easy bake that everyone loves!

Rosie

Chocolate Beetroot Cake

FOR THE SPONGE
200g salted butter, diced
100g 70% dark chocolate, broken into pieces
200g fresh, cooked beetroot in natural juice, finely grated
200g self-raising flour, sifted
1 teaspoon baking powder
50g dark cocoa powder
250g dark brown soft sugar
4 large eggs

FOR THE CHOCOLATE FUDGE ICING
200g condensed milk
½ teaspoon vanilla extract
50g unsalted butter, diced
100g 70% dark chocolate, chopped

YOU WILL NEED
18cm round cake tins x 2, greased, then base-lined with baking paper

1 Heat the oven to 180°C/160°C fan/350°F/Gas 4.

2 Place the butter in a medium pan over a low heat and heat gently for about 1 minute, until melted. Remove the pan from the heat and add the chocolate. Leave for 5 minutes, then stir until the chocolate has melted. Allow to cool for 10 minutes.

3 Place the beetroot in a large mixing bowl. Using a wooden spoon, stir in the flour, baking powder, cocoa, sugar and eggs, then stir in the cooled butter and chocolate mixture until fully combined.

4 Divide the mixture between the two cake tins and bake for 30–35 minutes, until a skewer inserted into the centres comes out clean. Leave to cool in the tins for 5 minutes, then turn out onto a wire rack to cool completely.

5 To make the icing, pour the condensed milk into a small pan with the vanilla and warm it over a low heat for 1–2 minutes, stirring continuously to prevent burning, until the milk is hot but not boiling. Remove the pan from the heat and add the butter and chocolate. Leave for 2–3 minutes, then stir until the butter and chocolate have melted and the mixture is smooth. Allow to cool until spreadable (about 1 hour).

6 When the icing is ready, spread one sponge, top-side down, evenly with half the icing. Stack the second sponge on top and spread with the remaining icing to finish.

SERVES
12

HANDS-ON
30 MINS

BAKE
1 HOUR

Amelia's recipe has evolved from her mum's much-loved carrot and apple muffins. Now a cake with cream cheese icing, it is a favourite with her work friends and makes the house smell lovely!

Carrot & Apple Cake

Amelia

FOR THE SPONGE
2 large firm, eating apples,
   peeled, cored and grated
100g carrots, peeled and grated
200g wholemeal plain flour
100g granulated sugar
2 tsp baking powder
1½ tsp ground cinnamon
1½ tsp ground ginger
¼ tsp salt
65ml runny honey
65ml maple syrup
165ml vegetable oil
3 eggs
1½ tsp vanilla extract
80g raisins
50g walnuts, chopped

FOR THE DECORATION
50g unsalted butter, softened
100g icing sugar, sifted
50ml double cream
100g full-fat cream cheese
50g walnuts, finely chopped
a pinch of ground cinnamon

YOU WILL NEED
20cm round, deep cake tin,
   greased, then base-lined
   with baking paper

1 Heat the oven to 180°C/160°C fan/350°F/Gas 4.

2 Put all the sponge ingredients in a mixing bowl. Using a wooden spoon, beat them together to make a soft batter. Pour the mixture into the prepared tin and bake for 1 hour, until golden brown, risen, and a skewer inserted into the centre comes out clean. Leave to cool in the tin for 10 minutes, then turn out onto a wire rack to cool completely.

3 To make the decoration, using an electric hand whisk, beat the butter in a bowl until really soft. Add the icing sugar and whisk on a low speed until combined and smooth. Add the double cream and whisk again for about 4 minutes, until thickened, then add the cream cheese and whisk again, briefly, until thick and creamy.

4 Spread the icing over the top and sides of the cake and sprinkle the walnuts on top. Finally, dust lightly with the pinch of cinnamon.

Priya's cake is inspired by a work friend's recipe. Overripe bananas add their own natural sweetness, and the optional extras – in this case pecans – make this recipe very easy to adapt.

Priya

Banana & Pecan Loaf

FOR THE SPONGE
100g unsalted butter, softened
100g demerara sugar
120g caster sugar
2 large eggs, beaten
3 overripe bananas
 (about 300g peeled
 weight), mashed
250g plain flour
1 tsp baking powder
½ tsp bicarbonate soda
½ tsp salt

FOR THE OPTIONAL EXTRAS
50g pecans, chopped,
 plus extra whole pecans
 for the top if you wish
50g walnuts, chopped,
 plus extra whole walnuts
 for the top if you wish
50g pitted dates, chopped

YOU WILL NEED
900g loaf tin, greased,
 then lined (base and sides)
 with baking paper

1 Heat the oven to 180°C/160°C fan/350°F/Gas 4.

2 Beat the butter and both sugars in a stand mixer fitted with the beater, on medium speed for about 5 minutes, until pale and creamy. Add the eggs, little by little, mixing well between each addition.

3 Mix in the mashed bananas, then sift the flour, baking powder, bicarbonate of soda and salt over the top. Fold them in using a large metal spoon.

4 Add any of the optional extras (pecans, walnuts and/or dates) you choose to make the cake your own, and stir them through until evenly distributed.

5 Pour the cake mixture into the prepared tin and add some nuts (if using) on top. Bake the cake for 1 hour, until golden, firm to the touch and a skewer inserted into the centre comes out clean. Leave to cool in the tin for 5 minutes, then transfer to a wire rack to cool completely.

Helena's lemon meringue cake comes from her great grandmother. Her family loves it so much that the siblings have to stake their claim straight after baking to ensure everyone gets their share!

Helena

Spanish Lemon Meringue Cake

250g digestive biscuits
110g unsalted butter, melted
5 eggs, separated
550g condensed milk
juice of 5 lemons
75g caster sugar

YOU WILL NEED
20cm round, loose-bottomed
  cake tin, greased, then
  lined (base and sides)
  with baking paper

1 Heat the oven to 200°C/180°C fan/400°F/Gas 6.

2 Blitz the biscuits in a food processor to fine crumbs. Remove 2 tablespoons of the crumbs and set aside. Add the melted butter to the crumbs in the food processor and blitz for a few seconds more until combined.

3 Transfer the buttery biscuit mixture to the prepared tin and use the back of a spoon to press it down firmly and evenly all the way to the edges of the tin to give an even base.

4 Place the egg yolks in a medium bowl. Using a balloon whisk, whisk in the condensed milk until fully incorporated. Then, slowly whisk in the lemon juice until combined. Pour the mixture on top of the biscuit base.

5 Place the egg whites in a clean, grease-free bowl and whisk with an electric hand whisk to stiff peaks. Whisk in the sugar, 1 tablespoon at a time, until the mixture forms a thick and glossy meringue. Spoon the meringue on top of the lemony layer in the tin.

6 Sprinkle the reserved biscuit mixture on top of the meringue and bake the lemon meringue cake for about 25 minutes, until the top is golden brown. Leave to cool in the tin for 30 minutes, then move it to the fridge to cool completely.

7 When you're ready to serve, release the cake from the tin, remove the baking paper and serve in slices.

This is a recipe passed down from Steph's great grandmother via her mum. A rich cake, soaked in brandy, it is best baked at least five weeks before eating. These quantities will also make a single 30cm cake, baked for 4–4½ hours.

Steph

Great Grandma's Christmas Fruitcake

FOR THE FRUIT CAKE
475g salted butter, softened
475g dark muscovado sugar
8 eggs, beaten
475g self-raising flour, sifted
1½ tsp mixed spice
¼ tsp nutmeg
a pinch of salt
500g raisins
500g currants
500g sultanas
75g each of green and red
   glacé cherries, quartered
125g candied peel, chopped
50g angelica, chopped
finely grated zest of
   1½ unwaxed lemons
2 tbsp brandy, plus extra
   for feeding the cake

FOR THE ALMOND PASTE
800g ground almonds
400g caster sugar
400g icing sugar, sifted
2 tbsp vanilla essence
juice of 2 lemons
3 eggs, beaten
6 tbsp homemade or
   good-quality apricot jam

FOR THE ROYAL ICING
4 egg whites
1kg icing sugar, sifted
4 tsp lemon juice
2 tsp glycerine

1 Heat the oven to 150°C/130°C fan/300°F/Gas 2.

2 Beat the butter and sugar in a stand mixer fitted with the beater, on medium speed for 5 minutes, until pale and creamy. With the mixer on a low speed, add the eggs, a little at a time, beating well between each addition.

3 Place the flour, spices, salt, raisins, currants, sultanas, glacé cherries, candied peel, angelica and lemon zest into a very large mixing bowl and stir together. Add the 2 tablespoons of brandy, then add the creamed mixture to the fruit and stir well with a large metal spoon until evenly combined.

4 Divide the mixture proportionately between the two tins. Level the tops, then bake: the 23cm cake will take 3½–4 hours and the 15cm will take about 2½ hours – or until the cakes feel firm to the touch, are a rich, golden brown, and a skewer inserted into centres comes out clean. If they are colouring too much, cover them with foil for the remaining baking time.

5 Once the cakes are baked, leave them to cool completely in the tins, then remove them onto a plate or board, leaving the baking paper attached to the sides and bottom to keep them moist. Don't worry if there's a little dip in the top of each cake.

6 Use a skewer to pierce the cakes all over, taking care not to pierce all the way to the bottom. Spoon 2 tablespoons of extra brandy into each cake, then cover the cakes with baking paper and wrap them in foil. Place them in a tin or box, to store.

7 Uncover the cakes once a week for the next 4 weeks, each time feeding with 1 tablespoon of brandy each.

YOU WILL NEED
23cm and 15cm round, deep
cake tins, greased then
double lined (base and sides)
with baking paper, then
double wrapped in strips
of brown paper around
the outsides of the tins
(tie with string)

8 About 1 week before you intend to serve the cakes, make the almond paste. In a bowl, using a wooden spoon, mix together the almonds, caster sugar and icing sugar. Add the vanilla, lemon juice and enough of the beaten eggs to give a stiff paste (you may not need all the egg). Chill the paste for 30 minutes to firm up.

9 For the 15cm cake you will need about 550g paste; for the 23cm cake about 950g. On a surface lightly dusted with icing sugar, roll out one half of each weighed portion of almond paste to a circle large enough to cover the top of each cake and about 1–1.5cm thick. With the remaining paste, roll out two long strips, one each to cover the sides of the cakes.

10 Heat the apricot jam in a small pan over a low heat to loosen. Brush the top and side of each cake with the warm jam, then place the appropriate circle of almond paste on top and wrap the appropriate strip around the side, trimming any excess and pressing the seam together where the pieces of paste meet. Loosely cover the cakes with baking paper and leave for at least 24 hours before adding the royal icing.

11 To make the royal icing, whisk the egg whites with an electric hand whisk for about 1–2 minutes, until frothy. Whisk in the icing sugar and stir in the lemon juice and glycerine. Whisk together until the icing is thick enough to hold stiff peaks.

12 Using a palette knife, spread the tops and sides of the cakes with royal icing. Smooth it around the sides and rough up the tops to create a snow effect. Leave the cakes overnight at room temperature to allow the icing to harden, then store in a tin or box until needed. (Don't wrap the cakes in cling film or use a plastic box as they will go mouldy.)

Photos overleaf

Inspired by the show, Michelle first made this cake five years ago for her husband's birthday – now it is a regular feature at family celebrations. She changes the jam flavour according to what's in season. Tonka beans give a warming, spiced flavour to the custard.

Seasonal Prinsesstårta

Michelle

FOR THE TONKA-BEAN CUSTARD
300ml whole milk
4 tonka beans, finely grated
½ tsp vanilla paste
3 egg yolks
50g caster sugar
25g cornflour
25g unsalted butter

FOR THE BLACKBERRY & APPLE JAM
200g blackberries
1 Braeburn or Cox apple, peeled, cored and grated
4 bay leaves
300g jam sugar

FOR THE SPONGE
4 large eggs
150g caster sugar
75g cornflour, sifted
75g plain flour, sifted
1 tsp baking powder
50g unsalted butter, melted

FOR THE FILLING
600ml double cream

FOR THE MARZIPAN
200g ground almonds
75g caster sugar
125g icing sugar, sifted
1 egg
1 tsp almond extract
purple food-colouring paste

Continues overleaf

1 For the custard, pour the milk into a pan with the grated tonka beans and the vanilla paste and place over a low heat for 2–3 minutes, until just simmering. Remove from the heat and set aside. In a large bowl, whisk the egg yolks, sugar and cornflour together until pale and creamy.

2 Strain the milk through a sieve and discard the tonka beans. Stir the warm milk slowly into the egg mixture. Pour the mixture back into the pan and cook over a low heat for 4–5 minutes, whisking, until the mixture thickens. (It should be very thick.) Remove the pan from the heat and beat in the butter until melted and incorporated. Transfer the custard to a bowl, cover the surface with cling film to prevent a skin forming, leave to cool, then place in the fridge to chill.

3 For the jam, tip the blackberries, apple and bay leaves into a medium pan with the sugar. Cook gently over a low heat, stirring occasionally, for 3–4 minutes, until the sugar has dissolved. Increase the heat and boil vigorously for about 4 minutes, or until the temperature reaches 104°C/219°F on a sugar thermometer. Transfer the mixture to a heatproof bowl and leave to cool completely.

4 Heat the oven to 180°C/160°C fan/350°F/Gas 4.

5 Make the sponge. Whisk the eggs and sugar in a stand mixer fitted with the whisk, on high speed until thick and mousse-like, and the mixture leaves a ribbon trail when you lift the whisk.

6 Add the cornflour, flour and baking powder over the egg mixture and carefully fold in using a large metal spoon. Fold in the melted butter, taking care not to over-mix.

Continues overleaf

TO DECORATE
edible flowers or a sugar-craft
    flower garland

YOU WILL NEED
sugar thermometer
23cm springform tin,
    greased, then base-lined
    with baking paper
medium piping bag fitted
    with a small plain nozzle
cocktail stick

7 Pour the mixture into the prepared tin and bake for 25–30 minutes, until the sponge is golden and is just shrinking away from the sides. Cool in the tin for 5–10 minutes, then turn out onto a wire rack to cool completely.

8 To assemble the cake, using a serrated knife, cut the sponge horizontally into three even layers. Place one layer onto a serving plate. Remove the custard from the fridge and spread a very thin layer over the base of the first sponge.

9 Spoon one quarter of the remaining custard into the piping bag fitted with the plain nozzle and pipe a border around the edge of the sponge (as a 'wall' for the jam). Spread about 5 tablespoons of jam over the sponge within the border. (You won't need all the jam – save the rest for spreading on toast.)

10 In a bowl, using an electric hand whisk, whip the double cream for the filling until firm. Fold half the whipped cream into the remaining custard from the fridge. Spread one third of the custard cream over the jam. Place the second sponge on top and spread over the remaining custard cream.

11 Place the third sponge on top. Spoon over the remaining whipped cream, covering the sides of the sponge and smoothing it into a small dome shape on the top. Chill the cake in the fridge for 1 hour.

12 Meanwhile, make the marzipan. Mix the ground almonds and sugars together in a stand mixer fitted with the dough hook. Add the egg and almond extract and mix to a stiff dough (this will take seconds). Turn out the marzipan onto a surface dusted with icing sugar. Using a cocktail stick, add a tiny amount of purple food colouring to the marzipan and knead it to an even colour.

13 Roll out the marzipan on a surface lightly dusted with icing sugar, into a circle (about 40cm in diameter) large enough to cover the cake. Lift the marzipan up over the cake and shape it around the sides to get a smooth finish. Trim away any excess. Decorate with edible or sugarcraft flowers.

Alice loves the combination of flavours in this cake – and the fact that you can easily double up the recipe to add layers and make something extra-impressive for a special occasion.

Alice

Pear & Hazelnut Cake

1 Heat the oven to 180°C/160°C fan/350°F/Gas 4.

2 In a large mixing bowl, whisk together the sugar, eggs and sunflower oil with a balloon whisk until smooth.

3 In a separate bowl, sift together the flour, baking powder and cocoa powder. Add the pears, chocolate and hazelnuts and toss together. Then, using a large metal spoon, fold the wet ingredients into the dry, until evenly combined.

4 Divide the mixture equally between the prepared tins and smooth the tops with the back of a spoon. Bake for about 20–25 minutes, or until just firm to the touch. Leave to cool in the tins for 10 minutes, then turn out onto a wire rack to cool completely.

5 While the cakes are baking, make the poached pears. Pour 400ml of water into a medium pan. Place over a medium heat and add the sugar, cinnamon and vanilla. Bring the mixture to the boil, then gently lower the pear halves into the sugar syrup, making sure they are fully submerged. Simmer the pears in the syrup for 5–7 minutes, testing occasionally with the point of a knife, until they are tender. Remove the pear halves with a slotted spoon and set aside to cool.

6 For the maple cream cheese icing, place the cream cheese and butter in a bowl and beat with a wooden spoon until very smooth. Gradually add the icing sugar, beating well after each addition, until the mixture is smooth and thick. Then, stir in the maple syrup.

7 Once the cakes have cooled, spread a thick layer of the icing on each cake. Thinly slice the pears and arrange the best slices on one of the cakes in a spiral. Put all the trimmings on the other cake. Stack the cakes one on top of the other, with the layer with the spiral of pears on top.

FOR THE SPONGE
220g light muscovado sugar
4 eggs
200ml sunflower oil
200g plain flour
2 tsp baking powder
50g cocoa powder
4 ripe pears, peeled, cored and cut into small chunks
150g 70% dark chocolate, finely chopped
150g toasted hazelnuts, finely chopped

FOR THE POACHED PEARS
100g caster sugar
1 tsp ground cinnamon
½ tsp vanilla paste
2 ripe pears, peeled, halved and cored

FOR THE MAPLE CREAM CHEESE ICING
125g full-fat cream cheese
125g unsalted butter, softened
250g icing sugar
1 tsp maple syrup

YOU WILL NEED
20cm sandwich tins x 2, greased, then base-lined with baking paper

This is a family recipe that has been passed down to Michael from his great grandmother via his grandmother and mum – in fact, it's one of the first cakes he and his mum ever baked together.

Michael

Sticky Gingerbread Loaf

FOR THE SPONGE
250g plain flour
4 tsp ground ginger
140ml whole milk
1 tsp bicarbonate of soda
100g sunflower spread
100g dark muscovado sugar
100g golden syrup
100g black treacle
1 egg

FOR THE ICING
150g icing sugar, sifted
4–5 tsp lemon juice

YOU WILL NEED
900g loaf tin, greased,
   then lined (base and sides)
   with baking paper

1 Heat the oven to 160°C/140°C fan/315°F/Gas 2–3.

2 Sift the flour and ginger together into a large mixing bowl and set aside. Measure 1 tablespoon of the milk into a small bowl and stir in the bicarbonate of soda.

3 Pour the remaining milk, along with the spread, sugar, syrup and treacle into a medium pan and place over a medium heat for about 2 minutes, until the spread has melted.

4 Leave the spread mixture to cool for 5 minutes, then pour it into the bowl over the flour and ginger. Add the egg, and the bicarbonate of soda mixture and beat with a wooden spoon to a smooth, thick batter.

5 Pour the batter into the prepared tin and bake for 50–60 minutes, or until a skewer inserted into the centre comes out clean. Leave to cool in the tin for 5 minutes, then transfer to a wire rack to cool completely.

6 Mix the icing sugar with enough lemon juice to make a thick pouring consistency. Once the cake is cool, drizzle the icing over the cake to finish.

A few years ago, Jamie's grandma brought him a liquorice birthday cake. He loved it so much, he decided to make his own. Keep the liquorice icing fairly thick to stop it running all down the sides.

Jamie

Liquorice Sponge Cake

FOR THE SPONGE
300g unsalted butter
150g caster sugar
150g light muscovado sugar
6 eggs, beaten
300g plain flour, sifted
1 tsp baking powder
1½ tbsp liquorice essence
shavings of white chocolate,
   to decorate

FOR THE BUTTERCREAM
75g salted butter, softened
150g icing sugar, sifted
25g cocoa powder

FOR THE LIQUORICE ICING
150g fondant icing sugar
1 tsp liquorice essence
black food-colouring gel

YOU WILL NEED
20cm sandwich tins x 2,
   greased, then base-lined
   with baking paper

1 Heat the oven to 180°C/160°C fan/350°F/Gas 4.

2 Beat the butter and sugars in a stand mixer fitted with the beater, on medium speed for 3–5 minutes, until pale and creamy. Add the eggs, little by little, beating well between each addition.

3 Using a metal spoon, fold in the flour, baking powder and liquorice essence until combined. Divide the mixture between the two prepared tins and bake for 35–40 minutes, until a skewer inserted into the centres comes out clean. Leave to cool in the tins for 5 minutes, then turn out onto a wire rack to cool completely.

4 Make the buttercream. Place the butter in a mixing bowl and beat with an electric hand whisk until fluffy. Gradually add the icing sugar and cocoa powder, and beat until fully combined. Spread the buttercream on one of the cooked cakes and place the other cake on top.

5 To make the liquorice icing, mix the icing sugar with the liquorice essence and enough water to make a thick, pouring consistency. Mix in the black food colouring to turn the icing completely black. Pour the icing over the top of the cake and decorate with white chocolate shavings to finish.

This was David's favourite recipe when he was growing up – he's always been obsessed with the flavour of almonds. His mum packed the cake with poppy seeds, too, to make it that bit healthier.

David

Almond Poppy Seed Cake

FOR THE SPONGE
85g poppy seeds
160ml whole milk
3 eggs
170g caster sugar
110ml light olive oil
1 tbsp good-quality
   almond essence
200g plain flour, sifted
1 tsp baking powder
60g ground almonds

FOR THE ALMOND GLAZE
100g icing sugar, sifted
½ tsp good-quality
   almond essence
25g flaked almonds

YOU WILL NEED
1.5 litre bundt tin or ring
   mould, well greased

1 Heat the oven to 180°C/160°C fan/350°F/Gas 4.

2 Put the poppy seeds and milk into a pan over a medium-high heat. As soon as the milk comes to the boil remove the pan from the heat and allow the mixture to cool.

3 In a medium bowl, mix the eggs and the sugar with an electric hand whisk for 3–4 minutes, until thick and creamy. Little by little, pour in the olive oil and then the almond essence, whisking between each addition, until combined.

4 Whisk in the flour, baking powder and ground almonds, and finally the milk and poppy-seed mixture, whisking until you have a thick batter.

5 Pour the batter into the prepared tin and bake for 30–35 minutes, or until skewer inserted into the ring comes out clean. Leave to cool in the tin for 5 minutes, then transfer to a wire rack to cool completely.

6 While the cake is cooling, make the glaze. Mix the icing sugar and almond essence together with about 1–2 tablespoons of water to give a thick, pouring consistency. Drizzle the icing over the cooled cake.

7 Toast the flaked almonds in a dry frying pan until lightly golden brown, then sprinkle these over the icing to finish.

CHAPTER FOUR

Fruit & Nut

This fruit cake is a keeper. Double wrap it in baking paper, then in foil and store it for up to 3 months, feeding it with extra brandy to help it mature (it will also freeze for up to 6 months). Use the table over the page for alternative sizes.

Traditional Fruit Cake

200g natural-coloured glacé
    cherries, washed and halved
200g sultanas
275g raisins
275g currants
75g mixed peel
150g unsalted butter, diced
150g molasses sugar
175g plain flour, sifted
½ tsp ground cinnamon
½ tsp ground ginger
¼ tsp ground nutmeg
a pinch of ground cloves
½ tsp mixed spice
3 eggs, beaten
175ml brandy, plus 120ml
    to pour (and extra to feed,
    if necessary)

YOU WILL NEED
20cm round, deep cake tin,
    greased, then lined (base
    and sides) with baking paper
extra baking paper and foil,
    for wrapping

1 Heat the oven to 160°C/140°C fan/315°F/Gas 2–3.

2 Place the dried fruit and peel into a large bowl (big enough to hold the entire mixture, once the butter and flour are added, too) and stir with a large spoon until everything is evenly distributed.

3 Melt the butter and molasses in a non-stick pan over a low heat for 2–3 minutes, stirring occasionally.

4 Stir the flour and spices into the fruit mixture, then add the warm butter and sugar mixture. Add the eggs and brandy, and stir again to combine. Spoon the mixture into the prepared tin and level it with the back of a spoon.

5 Bake the cake for 1 hour, then reduce the temperature to 140°C/120°C fan/275°F/Gas 1 and bake for a further 1 hour, or until a skewer inserted into the centre comes out pasty (but not wet).

6 Remove the cake from the oven and pierce it all over with a skewer. Pour the additional brandy over the top and leave the cake to cool in the tin completely.

7 Once the cake is cold, remove it from the tin along with the lining paper. Wrap the cake in the lining paper, and another two layers of baking paper and then in foil. Store the cake in a box (not an airtight plastic container) for up to 3 months in a cool, dry place. Feed with brandy from time to time, if you like.

SCALING QUANTITIES
TRADITIONAL FRUIT CAKE

All these versions of the Classic Fruit Cake will give you a delicious 5cm-deep cake (either round or loaf) – except for the traybake, which will be a more bitesize 2.5cm deep and is perfect for snacking or lunchboxes.

	25cm round, deep cake tin	30cm round, deep cake tin	900g loaf tin	23 x 30cm traybake tin
natural-coloured glacé cherries, washed and halved	315g	450g	150g	240g
sultanas	315g	450g	150g	240g
raisins	430g	620g	200g	330g
currants	430g	620g	200g	330g
mixed peel	115g	165g	50g	85g
unsalted butter, diced	250g	360g	125g	200g
molasses sugar	250g	360g	125g	200g
plain flour, sifted	300g	430g	150g	275g
ground cinnamon	1½ tsp	2 tsp	½ tsp	1 tsp
ground ginger	1½ tsp	2 tsp	½ tsp	1 tsp
ground nutmeg	½ tsp	1 tsp	¼ tsp	½ tsp
ground cloves	good pinch	good pinch	pinch	good pinch
mixed spice	1½ tsp	2 tsp	½ tsp	1 tsp
eggs, beaten	5	7	2	4
brandy	275ml	390ml	125ml	200ml
Baking time @ 160°C/ 140°C fan/315°F/Gas 2–3	1 hour, then reduce oven to 140°C/ 120°C fan/ 275°F/Gas 1 for 1 hour 15–20 mins	1 hour, then reduce oven to 140°C/ 120°fan/275°F/ Gas 1 for 1 hour 30–40 mins (cover with baking paper for the final 30–40 mins)	1 hour 15 mins	1 hour

Don't be put off by the longer baking and cooling times for this cake – it's really simple to make. Dusting the fruit in flour before folding in helps to prevent the berries sinking in the mixture.

Blackberry Pound Cake

FOR THE SPONGE
250g unsalted butter, softened
    at room temperature
425g golden caster sugar
1 tsp vanilla paste
5 eggs
180ml whole milk
340g plain flour, sifted, plus
    an extra 1 tbsp for dusting
2 tsp baking powder
a pinch of salt
225g blackberries

FOR THE TOPPING
350g thick Greek yogurt
1 tbsp runny honey
100g blackberries, halved
edible flowers (optional)

YOU WILL NEED
23cm deep, round cake tin,
    greased, then lined (base
    and sides) with baking paper

1 Heat the oven to 180°C/160°C fan/350°F/Gas 4.

2 Beat the butter, sugar and vanilla in a stand mixer fitted with the beater, on medium speed for 2–3 minutes, until pale and creamy.

3 With the mixer on a low speed, add the eggs, one at a time, beating well between each addition (don't worry if the mixture curdles slightly – it will come together when you add the flour).

4 Gradually add the milk and mix well to combine. Using a large metal spoon, fold the flour, baking powder and salt into the mixture, until just combined.

5 Put the blackberries in a small plastic bag with the extra 1 tablespoon of flour and give them a shake to coat. Gently fold them into the cake mixture until evenly distributed.

6 Pour the mixture into the prepared tin and bake for 50–60 minutes, until golden brown and a skewer inserted into the centre comes out clean. Turn out onto a wire rack and leave to cool completely (about 1–2 hours).

7 Meanwhile, make the topping. Using a wooden spoon, beat together the Greek yogurt and honey in a bowl, until smooth.

8 Once the cake is completely cool, spread the topping on top. Decorate with the halved blackberries and then dot with edible flowers, if using.

This cake, Edd's creation from Series 1, is light and airy – think dreamy gâteau, rather than a more filling banana bread.

Caramel, Cinnamon & Banana Cake

Edd

FOR THE CARAMEL
200g caster sugar
200ml whipping cream
15g unsalted butter

FOR THE SPONGE
8 large eggs
300g light brown soft sugar
200g plain flour
20g cornflour
1 tbsp ground cinnamon
½ tsp ground nutmeg
40g unsalted butter,
    melted and cooled
6 walnuts halves,
    roughly chopped
6 dried banana chips,
    roughly chopped
1 small banana
2 tbsp granulated sugar

FOR THE SYRUP
50g caster sugar
1½ tbsp vanilla extract

FOR THE CARAMEL ICING
125g caster sugar
3 egg whites, at room
    temperature
a pinch of cream of tartar
225g unsalted butter,
    at room temperature
1 quantity of caramel (above)

YOU WILL NEED
20cm sandwich tins x 3,
    greased, then base-lined
    with baking paper
kitchen blowtorch
sugar thermometer

1 For the caramel, tip the sugar into a heavy-based pan and melt over a medium–low heat. Increase the heat and cook until golden-amber (about 3–4 minutes). Remove from the heat and carefully add one third of the cream (take care as it will spit). Once the bubbling has subsided, whisk in the remaining cream, then stir in the butter until smooth and thick. Leave to cool in a shallow dish, then place in the fridge to chill.

2 Heat the oven to 180°C/160°C fan/350°F/Gas 4.

3 For the sponge, place the eggs and sugar in a bowl set over a pan of simmering water. Using an electric hand whisk, whisk to melt the sugar.

4 Transfer the mixture to a stand mixer fitted with the whisk and whisk on high speed until the mixture is thick and mousse-like, and leaves a ribbon trail when you lift the whisk.

5 Sift together the flour, cornflour, cinnamon and nutmeg. Sift one third over the egg mixture and fold in with a large metal spoon. Repeat, folding in the remaining flour mixture one third at a time, until there is no trace of flour in the mixture.

6 Divide the mixture evenly between the three tins and bake for 15 minutes, until a skewer inserted into the centres comes out clean. Cool in the tins for 10 minutes, then turn out onto a wire rack to cool completely.

7 For the syrup, heat the sugar with 120ml of water in a pan over a low heat, stirring until the sugar has dissolved. Boil until reduced by half (about 2–3 minutes). Remove from the heat and stir in the vanilla extract. Leave to cool.

Continues overleaf

8 For the caramel icing, tip the sugar into a pan with 50ml of water and cook over medium heat until the syrup reaches 114°C/237°F on the sugar thermometer.

9 Whisk together the egg whites and cream of tartar in a stand mixer fitted with a whisk, on high speed until they form stiff peaks. Whisking continuously, pour the syrup down the side of the bowl, then continue whisking for 3–5 minutes, until the mixture is cool enough not to melt the butter. Add the butter a little at a time, whisking well between each addition, to a thick, smooth, creamy icing.

10 Still whisking continuously, add the cooled caramel one quarter at a time, until light and fluffy.

11 To assemble, brush the sponges with the cooled syrup. Place one of the sponges on a cake plate and spread with one quarter of the caramel icing. Top with the second sponge and spread with another quarter of the caramel icing. Top with the third sponge, then cover the top and sides of the cake with the remaining icing.

12 Sprinkle the chopped walnuts and banana chips around the edge of the cake, then cut the banana into 8, 10 or 12 slices (depending on the size of the banana). Place the slices on a baking tray and sprinkle with the sugar. Using a blowtorch, caramelise the sugar, then place the sticky banana slices on the cake to decorate.

Jo's chocolate and orange cupcakes (from Series 2) use a classic pairing, but it's also easy to give them an alternative flavour. Substitute the orange syrup for chocolate, coffee or vanilla, if you prefer.

Jo

Chocolate & Orange Cupcakes

FOR THE CUPCAKES
50g 70% dark chocolate,
    broken into pieces
120g plain flour, sifted
1 tsp baking powder
140g caster sugar
40g unsalted butter,
    softened and diced
1 large egg
120ml whole milk,
    at room temperature
1 unwaxed orange
3 tbsp granulated sugar
chocolate shavings,
    to decorate

FOR THE BUTTERCREAM
4 tbsp whole milk
50g white chocolate
125g unsalted butter, softened
500g icing sugar, sifted

YOU WILL NEED
12-hole muffin tray,
    lined with cupcake cases
cocktail stick
large piping bag fitted with
    a large closed star nozzle

1 Heat the oven to 180°C/160°C fan/350°F/Gas 4. Melt the chocolate in a bowl set over a pan of simmering water. Remove from the pan and stir until smooth, then leave to cool.

2 Tip the flour, baking powder and caster sugar into a food processor and pulse to mix. Add the butter and process to a sandy texture. Mix the egg into the milk then, with the machine running, slowly add the mixture through the feed tube. Scrape down the sides, add the melted chocolate and run the machine until the mixture is thoroughly combined.

3 Divide the mixture equally between the cupcake cases, then bake for 15–20 minutes, or until just firm to the touch.

4 Meanwhile, grate the zest from half the orange and reserve for decoration. Pare a long strip of peel from the remaining half and reserve for the buttercream. Juice the orange into a bowl and mix in the granulated sugar until dissolved.

5 Pierce the hot cupcakes in several places with the cocktail stick. Spoon the orange syrup over and leave for 5 minutes to soak in, then cool the cupcakes in their cases on a wire rack.

6 For the buttercream, heat the milk in a small pan until just below boiling. Remove from the heat and add the orange peel. Leave to infuse until the milk is cold, then discard the peel. Melt the white chocolate in a bowl set over a pan of simmering water. Stir until smooth, then leave to cool.

7 Using an electric hand whisk, beat the butter in a bowl until creamy. Slowly beat in the icing sugar and the cooled milk, then beat in the cooled, melted chocolate, until smooth.

8 Spoon the icing into the large piping bag fitted with the star nozzle. Pipe the buttercream onto the cupcakes in swirls and top with orange zest and chocolate shavings.

A glorious celebration of summer, this cake is topped with edible flowers – feel free to choose your favourites. The gooseberry compote is best made the day before you intend to bake.

Gooseberry & Elderflower Cake

FOR THE GOOSEBERRY COMPOTE
500g gooseberries, topped, tailed and halved
100g granulated sugar
5 heads of elderflower (optional)

FOR THE SPONGE
8 large eggs
465g unsalted butter, softened
465g caster sugar
465g self-raising sponge flour, sifted
4 tsp baking powder
small, edible meadow flowers, with stems, to decorate

FOR THE ELDERFLOWER & ROSE SYRUP
200g granulated sugar
6 tbsp elderflower & rose cordial

FOR THE ELDERFLOWER & ROSE BUTTERCREAM
350g unsalted butter
¾ tsp fine salt
¾ tsp white vinegar
6 tbsp elderflower & rose cordial
1.35kg icing sugar, sifted
150g double cream

Continues overleaf

1 For the gooseberry compote, place the gooseberries in a deep-sided pan with 50ml of water and the sugar. Tie the elderflowers (if using) in a small piece of muslin and add to the pan. Bring to the boil, reduce the heat and simmer for 15 minutes until the gooseberries are tender. Remove from the heat and carefully pour into a shallow container. Leave to cool, then chill to set.

2 For the sponges, heat the oven to 190°C/170°C fan/375°F/ Gas 5. Beat all the sponge ingredients, except the flowers, in a stand mixer fitted with the beater, on medium speed for 2 minutes, until smooth.

3 Measure about 250g of the sponge mixture into each of the two 15cm tins and about 400g into each of the 20cm tins. Bake the 15cm sponges for about 20 minutes and the 20cm sponges for 25–30 minutes, until springy to the touch. Remove from the oven and leave to cool in the tins.

4 For the elderflower and rose syrup, tip the sugar into a pan. Add 200ml of water and bring to the boil over a gentle heat, stirring to melt the sugar. Boil for 3–5 minutes, until reduced to a syrup consistency or the temperature on a sugar thermometer reaches 110°C/230°F. Remove from the heat, stir in the cordial and set aside to cool until warm.

5 Using a cocktail stick, poke small holes all over the sponges and spoon over three quarters of the warm (but not hot) elderflower syrup. Leave the sponges in the tins to cool completely.

6 For the elderflower and rose buttercream, beat the butter, salt, vinegar and cordial together in a stand mixer fitted with the beater, on medium–low speed for 2–3 minutes, until smooth.

Continues overleaf

Fruit & Nut **191**

YOU WILL NEED

15cm sandwich tins x 2,
   greased, then base-lined
20cm sandwich tins x 3,
   greased, then base-lined
sugar thermometer (optional)
cocktail stick
1 large piping bag fitted with
   a medium plain nozzle
20cm cake drum
3 x plastic cake dowels
15cm cake card

7 On a low speed, add half the icing sugar, then add half the double cream and beat for 3 minutes, until very smooth. Add in the remaining icing sugar and the remaining cream and continue beating on low speed for 3 minutes, until very smooth but not aerated. Spoon one quarter of the buttercream into the large piping bag fitted with the medium plain nozzle, leaving the remaining buttercream in the bowl.

8 To assemble, trim the sponges level, if needed. Pipe a dot of buttercream onto the 20cm cake drum and top with a 20cm sponge. Brush the sponge with one fifth of the remaining syrup, then spread with one eighth of the buttercream. Pipe a line of buttercream around the edge of the sponge to act as a reservoir and fill with one third of the gooseberry compote.

9 Place the second 20cm sponge on top and repeat as in Step 8. Top with the third 20cm sponge, brush with syrup, then spread one eighth of the buttercream over the top. Space the dowels in a triangle formation in the middle of the cake, about 8cm apart, and push down through the sponges. Trim the dowels flush with the top of the cake.

10 Pipe a dot of buttercream onto the 15cm cake card and top with a 15cm sponge. Brush the sponge with one fifth of the remaining syrup, then spread with one eighth of the buttercream. Pipe a line of buttercream around the edge of the sponge to act as a reservoir and fill with the remaining compote. Brush the underside of the remaining sponge with the leftover syrup and place top-side up on the gooseberry compote. Spread with one eighth of the buttercream.

11 Using the remaining buttercream in the piping bag, spread a thin layer of buttercream over the sides of the cakes and smooth off to form a crumb coat. Then, using the remaining buttercream in the bowl, repeat the crumb-coating process to create a semi-naked effect with small patches of sponge peeping through. (You can scrape off more or less buttercream, according to the effect you want to create.)

12 Chill the cake until ready to serve, then decorate with edible flowers immediately before serving (the flowers can wilt quickly, so do this at the very last minute).

The filling of Beca's (Series 4) moist, zingy cake (think vibrant twist on a lemon drizzle) is made from cream and mascarpone, so store any uneaten cake in the fridge – it will keep for 2–3 days.

Beca

Grapefruit Sandwich Cake

FOR THE SPONGE
200g caster sugar
200g soft baking spread
4 large eggs
200g self-raising flour, sifted
25g ground almonds
finely grated zest of 1 unwaxed
    grapefruit and juice of ½

FOR THE GRAPEFRUIT SYRUP
juice of 1½ grapefruits
75g caster sugar

FOR THE GRAPEFRUIT CURD
finely grated zest of
    ½ unwaxed grapefruit
juice of 1½ grapefruits
50g unsalted butter
50g caster sugar
2 large eggs, beaten

FOR THE CANDIED PEEL
peel, but no pith of
    ½ unwaxed grapefruit,
    sliced into thin matchsticks
75g caster sugar, plus extra
    for sprinkling

FOR THE MASCARPONE CREAM
150g mascarpone
150g double cream
50g icing sugar

YOU WILL NEED
20cm sandwich tins x 2,
    greased, then base-lined
small piping bag fitted with
    a large writing nozzle
medium piping bag fitted
    with a medium plain nozzle

1 Heat the oven to 180°C/160°C fan /350°F/Gas 4. Beat the sugar, spread, eggs, flour, almonds, zest and juice in a stand mixer fitted with the beater, on medium speed for 2 minutes, until smooth. Divide the mixture equally between the two tins. Bake for 25–30 minutes, until springy and a skewer inserted into the centres comes out clean. Cool slightly in the tins while you make the syrup.

2 Place the juice and sugar in a medium pan and bring slowly to the boil, stirring occasionally until the sugar dissolves. Then, boil for 5 minutes, to thicken. Cool slightly, then using a cocktail stick, poke holes over the warm sponges and spoon the syrup over. Leave the soaked sponges to cool in the tins.

3 For the curd, put the zest, juice, butter and sugar in a bowl set over a pan of simmering water. Stir occasionally, until the butter has melted, then whisk in the beaten eggs. Gently whisk the mixture for about 10 minutes, or until very thick. Pour into a shallow dish and leave to cool, then chill until set. Spoon one quarter of the cooled curd into the small piping bag.

4 For the candied peel, boil the grapefruit peel in a large pan of water for 15 seconds, then drain. Return the peel to the pan with the sugar and 75ml of water. Boil for 8–10 minutes, then remove the peel to a wire rack. Sprinkle with caster sugar.

5 For the mascarpone cream, whisk the mascarpone, double cream and icing sugar together to stiff (but not too stiff) peaks. Spoon one quarter of the mixture into the medium piping bag.

6 To assemble, place one of the sponges on a cake plate or stand. Spread half of the remaining mascarpone cream onto the sponge. Spoon over the grapefruit curd, then top with the other sponge. Spread the remaining mascarpone cream on top, then pipe blobs of the mascarpone cream around the edge. Pipe dots of lemon curd over the mascarpone blobs, and decorate the centre of the cake with the candied peel.

This classic is named for the French word for strawberry. Although the baking and assembly are relatively easy, you'll need about 2 hours to chill the components, so give yourself plenty of time.

Fraisier Cake

FOR THE GÉNOISE
4 eggs
150g golden caster sugar
150g self-raising flour
60g unsalted butter, melted

FOR THE CRÈME PÂTISSIÈRE
600ml whole milk
2 tsp vanilla paste
4 eggs, plus 2 egg yolks
175g caster sugar
60g plain flour, sifted
60g cornflour, sifted
150g unsalted butter, diced

TO ASSEMBLE
600g strawberries
pink food-colouring paste (optional)
200g marzipan
100g 70% dark chocolate, melted

YOU WILL NEED
23cm springform tin, greased, then base-lined with baking paper
strip of acetate, cut to fit the side of the tin
medium disposable piping bag
23cm-diameter circle of cut card (optional)
sheet of baking paper

1 Heat the oven to 200°C/180°C fan/400°F/Gas 6.

2 To make the génoise, whisk together the eggs and sugar in a stand mixer fitted with the whisk, on high speed until very light, tripled in volume, and the mixture leaves a ribbon trail when you lift the whisk.

3 Sift two-thirds of the flour onto the mixture, then gently fold in with a metal spoon. Add the remaining flour and continue to fold in gently, retaining as much air as possible, but incorporating all the flour. Gently fold in the melted butter.

4 Pour the mixture into the prepared tin and bake for 20–25 minutes, until the sponge is pale golden brown and shrinking away from the edges of the tin. Cool in the tin for 5 minutes, then turn out onto a wire rack to cool completely.

5 To make the crème pâtissière, bring the milk and vanilla just to the boil in a pan over a medium heat. Meanwhile, in a separate bowl, whisk together the whole eggs, egg yolks, sugar and both flours until smooth and creamy.

6 Pour the milk onto the egg mixture, whisking continuously, then pour back into the pan and cook over a low heat for 7–8 minutes, stirring continuously, until thickened to a piping consistency. Remove the heat and stir in the butter.

7 Leave the mixture to cool slightly, then pour it into a bowl to cool completely. Press a layer of cling film onto the surface, to stop a skin from forming, then chill for 1 hour, to set.

8 When you're ready to assemble the cake, slice the cooled sponge in half horizontally to make two thin, equal layers.

9 Line the sides of the springform tin with the acetate. Place one sponge layer, cut side upwards, in the tin. With the back

Continues overleaf

of a spoon, gently squash the edges of the sponge to push it up against the acetate.

10 Choose 10–14 strawberries of the same height and size, hull and cut them in half lengthways. Arrange the strawberries cut sides facing outwards around the edge of the sponge, pointed ends upwards. Make sure the strawberries fit snugly.

11 Spoon the chilled crème pâtissière into the piping bag. Snip a 2cm hole in the end and pipe the crème all over the base to cover the sponge, carefully piping between the fruit to fill any gaps. Using a palette knife, push the crème up against the acetate. Reserve the remainder in the piping bag.

12 Reserve seven of the remaining strawberries to decorate, then hull and dice the rest and spread them evenly all over the layer of crème pâtissière. Pipe the remaining crème over the top of the berries and level it with a palette knife.

13 Gently place the remaining sponge layer on top, cut side upwards. Lightly press down to ensure the cake is firmly pressed against the acetate.

14 Knead a tiny amount of pink food colouring into the marzipan to achieve a pale pink colour (you could leave the marzipan natural-coloured if you prefer).

15 Roll out the marzipan on a surface lightly dusted with icing sugar to a 23cm circle and about 5mm thick, using the cake tin or the measured circle of card as a guide. Place the marzipan disc on top of the cake, then chill the cake for 30–45 minutes.

16 While the cake is chilling, dip the reserved strawberries into the melted dark chocolate and place them on the sheet of baking paper to set.

17 Decorate the top of the cake with the dipped strawberries, then release the tin and carefully remove the acetate just before serving.

SERVES	HANDS-ON	BAKE
70	**4** HOURS	**2** HOURS

Frances's winning wedding cake from Series 4 is as enchanting now as it was then – a beautiful combination of flavoured sponges, coated in lemony buttercream and decorated with flowers.

Midsummer Night's Dream Cake

Frances

FOR THE GINGER SPONGE
345g dark muscovado sugar
345g slightly salted butter
345g treacle
345g golden syrup
4 large eggs
750ml full-fat milk
675g self-raising flour
1 tbsp bicarbonate of soda
4 tbsp ground ginger
1 tbsp mixed spice
400g rhubarb, chopped

FOR THE SUNSHINE SPONGE
90g light muscovado sugar
1 large egg
75ml sunflower oil
100g self-raising flour
½ tbsp ground cinnamon
½ tsp bicarbonate of soda
100g carrots, peeled and grated
finely grated zest of
    ½ unwaxed orange
25g pistachios, chopped
75g tinned pineapple,
    drained and chopped
50g soft apricots, chopped

FOR THE LEMON SPONGE
325g slightly salted butter
325g caster sugar
5 large eggs, beaten
260g self-raising flour
65g ground almonds
finely grated zest of
    3 unwaxed lemons

Continues overleaf

1 Heat the oven to 190°C/170°C fan/375°F/Gas 5. Make the ginger sponge. In a large pan melt the sugar, butter, treacle and golden syrup together over a very low heat, stirring occasionally, until the butter has melted and the sugar has dissolved. Remove from the heat and cool for 10–15 minutes.

2 In a bowl, whisk the eggs and milk together until smooth. In a separate very large bowl, sift the flour, bicarbonate of soda, ground ginger and mixed spice together. Stir the warm butter and sugar mixture into the flour mixture, then gradually add the egg mixture and stir together well.

3 Divide the mixture between the two prepared 23cm tins, scatter the rhubarb pieces over the top and bake for 1 hour, until a skewer inserted into the centres comes out clean. Cool in the tins for 15 minutes, then turn out onto a wire rack to cool completely.

4 To make the sunshine sponge, mix the sugar, egg and oil together in a bowl. In a separate bowl, sift the flour, cinnamon and bicarbonate of soda together.

5 Fold the flour mixture into the egg mixture, then fold in the carrots, orange zest, pistachios, pineapple and apricots. Spoon the mixture into the prepared 10cm cake tin and bake for about 40 minutes, until a skewer inserted into the centre comes out clean. Cool in the tin for 15 minutes, then turn out onto a wire rack to cool completely.

6 To make the lemon sponge, beat the butter and sugar together in a bowl until pale and creamy. Gradually add the beaten eggs, a little at a time, beating well between each addition. If the mixture looks as if it might curdle, add a spoonful of the flour. Sift over the remaining flour and the ground almonds. Add the lemon zest and fold together.

Continues overleaf

FOR THE MARZIPAN BEES
½ egg, beaten
¼ tsp orange blossom
   honey, plus a little extra
finely grated zest of
   ¼ unwaxed orange
¼ tsp orange blossom water
¼ tsp vanilla extract
¼ tsp almond extract
65g icing sugar
65g ground almonds
5g 70% dark chocolate
about 36 flaked almonds
   (make sure they aren't
   chipped or broken)
edible gold leaf

**FOR THE LIMONCELLO
MERINGUE BUTTERCREAM**
600g caster sugar
200ml lemon juice
10 large egg whites
1kg unsalted butter,
   diced and softened
3 tbsp limoncello
2 tsp lemon extract

FOR THE CREAM CHEESE FILLING
400g full-fat cream cheese
200g icing sugar, sifted

FOR THE LEMON CAKE FILLING
500–600g raspberries

TO DECORATE
edible flowers
fresh fruit of your choice

7 Divide the mixture equally between the three 15cm cake tins and level the tops. Bake for 20–25 minutes, until a skewer inserted into the centres comes out clean. Cool in the tins for 5 minutes, then transfer to a wire rack to cool completely.

8 Make the marzipan for the bees. Whisk the egg, honey, orange zest and extracts together in a small bowl. Sift over the icing sugar and ground almonds and stir to a smooth dough. Chill for 10 minutes to firm up.

9 Divide the mixture into 18 even-sized pieces. Roll each one in the palm of your hands and shape into the body of a bee. Set aside on a plate.

10 Melt the dark chocolate in a small heatproof bowl in the microwave, on a very low setting, checking every 10 seconds, making sure it doesn't overheat. Dip the fine paintbrush into the chocolate and paint three stripes onto each bee and put two dots at one end to make eyes.

11 Brush the ends of the flaked almonds with honey then, using the paintbrush to help you, carefully stick on a little gold leaf to each. Attach to the bodies to resemble wings. Set aside.

12 Make the buttercream (you may need to do this in two batches, using half the ingredients each time). Place 500g sugar into a medium heavy-based saucepan. Pour in the lemon juice and place over a low heat, swirling the pan to dissolve the sugar completely. When the syrup has turned clear, increase the heat to medium and boil the syrup to 121°C/250°F on the sugar thermometer.

13 Meanwhile, whisk the egg whites and the remaining 100g sugar in a stand mixer fitted with the whisk attachment until it forms stiff peaks.

14 Pour the hot sugar syrup into the meringue in a thin, steady steam. Once the syrup is fully combined, whisk for a further 5–8 minutes, until cool. With the mixer running, add the butter, a little at a time, then add the limoncello and lemon extract, until thick and creamy-white. Set aside until ready to use.

YOU WILL NEED

23cm round, deep cake tins x 2,
    greased, then lined (base and
    sides) with baking paper
10cm round, deep cake tin,
    greased, then lined (base
    and sides) with baking paper
15cm round, deep cake tins x 3,
    greased, then lined (base and
    sides) with baking paper
fine cake-decorating paintbrush
sugar thermometer
28cm cake drum
15cm cake card
10cm cake card
5 or 6 cake dowels
crank-handled palette knife

15 Make the cream cheese filling. Put the cream cheese into a large bowl with the icing sugar. Fold everything together to fully combine and set aside in the fridge to chill.

16 Assemble the cakes. Remove the paper from all the sponges. Trim the ginger cakes to neaten. Spread a little bit of buttercream in the middle of the cake drum, then put one ginger sponge on top. Spread the cream cheese filling over the top of the cake and top with the other ginger sponge. Spread a thin layer of buttercream over the top and sides, then chill for 10–15 minutes.

17 Trim the lemon cakes to neaten. Spread a little buttercream onto the larger cake card, then top with a lemon sponge. Spread buttercream over the top of the cake, top with half the raspberries then layer up the other two cakes with buttercream and raspberries, finishing with a thin layer of buttercream on the top cake. Spread a thin layer of buttercream round the outside. Lift onto a plate and chill for 10–15 minutes.

18 Trim the sunshine cake, put it on the smallest cake card and spread a thin layer of the buttercream over the top and sides. Chill the cake for 10–15 minutes.

19 Take the cakes out of the fridge. Cut three dowels to the height of the assembled ginger cake and push into the middle, in a well-spaced triangle formation.

20 Cut the remaining three cake dowels to the height of the lemon cake and push them into the middle of the lemon cake, again in a well-spaced triangle formation.

21 Lift the lemon cake on top of the ginger cake and put the sunshine cake on top. Using the palette knife, spread the remaining buttercream all over the cake, smoothing it out as you go. Decorate with edible flowers, fresh fruit and the bees.

Cakes don't come much more uplifting than this tropical fruit cake. It is packed with dried fruits for a natural sweetness that helps to keep down the refined sugar.

Sunshine Fruit Cake

FOR THE SPONGE
75g dried mango, diced
75g dried papaya, diced
100g dried apricots, snipped
50g sultanas
50g dried pineapple, diced
300ml tropical fruit juice
175g unsalted butter, softened
175g caster sugar
3 large eggs, beaten
200g plain flour
1 tsp baking powder
50g cornflour
finely grated zest of
    1 unwaxed lime
50g blanched almonds,
    roughly chopped

FOR THE CANDIED PEEL
peeled zest of ½ unwaxed
    lemon, cut into matchsticks
peeled zest of ½ unwaxed lime,
    cut into matchsticks
150g caster sugar, plus
    3 tbsp for dredging

FOR THE MARZIPAN FRUITS
125g icing sugar, sifted,
    plus extra if necessary
125g ground almonds
1 egg yolk
½ tsp vanilla extract
yellow food-colour paste
orange food-colouring paste
brown food-colouring paste
green food-colouring paste
purple food-colouring paste

Continues overleaf

1 Heat the oven to 170°C/150°C fan/325°F/Gas 3.

2 Place the mango, papaya, apricots, sultanas and pineapple in a bowl. Pour the tropical fruit juice into a pan and bring just to the boil. Pour the juice over the fruit and leave to cool to room temperature.

3 Beat the butter and sugar in a stand mixer fitted with the beater, on medium speed for 3–5 minutes, until pale and creamy. Add the eggs, a little at a time, beating well between each addition.

4 In a separate bowl, sift together the flour, baking powder and cornflour, then fold the dry mixture into the wet mixture, along with the lime zest.

5 Drain the cooled fruit mixture, giving the sieve a good tap to remove any excess juice, then fold the mixture into the sponge batter until well combined. Spoon the sponge mixture into the prepared tin and sprinkle over the chopped almonds. Bake for 1 hour 15 minutes, until a skewer inserted in the centre comes out clean. Leave to cool in the tin for 15 minutes, then transfer to a wire rack to cool completely.

6 For the candied peel, bring a small pan of water to the boil. Add the lemon and lime peel and boil for 5 minutes. Drain and return the peel to the pan. Add the sugar and 150ml of water and place over a low heat, stirring occasionally, until the sugar has melted. Simmer for 20–30 minutes, until translucent, then drain well and place the peel on a sheet of baking paper. Dredge with the extra 3 tablespoons of sugar and leave to dry.

7 For the marzipan fruits, beat together the icing sugar, ground almonds, egg yolk and vanilla in a stand mixer fitted with the beater, on a low speed until well combined. If the marzipan is too dry, add a little water; if it's too sticky add extra icing sugar.

Continues overleaf

FOR THE TROPICAL ICING
100g icing sugar
1–2 tbsp tropical fruit juice
pink food-colouring gel

FOR THE TOPPING
15g blanched almonds,
    roughly chopped and toasted
15g coconut flakes, toasted

YOU WILL NEED
900g loaf tin, greased,
    then lined (base and sides)
    with baking paper
craft knife
cake-decorating paintbrush
cocktail umbrellas (optional)

8 Shape the marzipan into little fruits – 2 oranges, 2 passion fruits, 2 bananas and 2 pineapples – using food colouring and a craft knife to add colour and detail. For example, try little crosses in the tops of the oranges with a little brown 'stud'; purple, spherical passion fruits, halved and painted yellow inside with little black spots; brown lines painted down the lengths of the yellow bananas, joined at the top with a little brown stem; and scored diagonal lines on the yellow pineapples, with small, green shoots for a top. Set aside.

9 For the tropical icing, sift the icing sugar into a bowl and gradually add the fruit juice, mixing to a dropping consistency (you may not need all the juice). Add a tiny drop of pink food colouring to colour the icing very pale pink.

10 Drizzle the icing over the cake, then sprinkle over the toasted almonds and coconut flakes for the topping. Decorate with the marzipan fruits, candied peel – and cocktail umbrellas, if you wish.

Liam's illusion masterpiece was a real highlight of Series 8 and would make a fantastic celebration showstopper for someone whose love of blueberry breakfast pancakes is equalled only by a love of delicious cake.

Stackin' Sunday Cake

Liam

FOR THE GRANOLA CRUMBLE
150g pecans, roughly chopped,
    plus 50g extra for sprinkling
60g plain flour, sifted
60g porridge oats
30g wheat germ
1 tsp salt
100g unsalted butter,
    chilled and diced
100g light muscovado sugar
50g demerara sugar
100g raisins

FOR THE SPONGE
3 tbsp buttermilk
1 tsp vanilla extract
1 overripe banana
250g self-raising flour
¾ tsp bicarbonate of soda
½ tsp ground nutmeg
1 tsp ground cinnamon
¼ tsp salt
220g unsalted butter, softened
165g caster sugar
55g light brown soft sugar
4 large eggs, beaten

FOR THE SWISS MERINGUE BUTTERCREAM
4 large egg whites
300g light brown soft sugar
400g unsalted butter, diced,
    at room temperature
½ tsp vanilla extract
4 tbsp Spanish forest honey

1 To make the granola crumble, tip the 150g pecans into a food processor and blitz to a large crumb. Tip the flour into a separate bowl, add the blitzed pecans along with the porridge oats, wheat germ, salt, butter and both sugars. Rub the butter in with your fingertips, until you have large chunks of crumble. Tip out onto the lined baking tray and set aside.

2 Heat the oven to 180°C/160°C fan/350°F/Gas 4. To make the sponge, tip the buttermilk, vanilla and banana into a food processor and blitz until smooth. In a separate bowl, sift the flour, bicarbonate of soda, nutmeg, cinnamon and salt together.

3 Cream the butter and sugar together in a stand mixer fitted with the beater, on high speed for 4–5 minutes, until pale and creamy. Add the eggs, little by little, beating well between each addition. If the mixture begins to split, add a tablespoon of the flour mixture and beat again.

4 With the mixer on a low speed, add the buttermilk mixture and the flour mixture, one third at a time, beating well between each addition, until combined. Divide equally between the three prepared tins and smooth with a palette knife.

5 Bake the sponges and crumble mixture for 25–30 minutes, until a skewer inserted into the centre of each sponge comes out clean and the crumble is deep golden brown. Remove from the oven and leave the sponges to cool in the tins for 15 minutes, then transfer to a wire rack to cool completely.

6 Leave the crumble to cool, then tip it into a food processor and pulse to large crumb. Stir in the raisins and the extra 50g of pecans and set aside.

FOR THE BLUEBERRY COMPOTE
400g frozen blueberries
2 tbsp Spanish forest honey
4 tsp cornflour

FOR THE FONDANT PANCAKES
450g white mini marshmallows
cream food-colouring gel
825g icing sugar, sifted
vegetable baking fat,
    for greasing
cornflour, for dusting
edible glue

TO DECORATE
cream food-colouring gel
golden yellow food-
    colouring gel
brown food-colouring gel
7 tbsp vodka

FOR THE CREAM
300ml double cream
icing sugar, for dusting

YOU WILL NEED
baking tray, lined
    with baking paper
15cm round cake tins x 3,
    greased, then lined
    (base and sides)
    with baking paper
kitchen string

7 To make the Swiss meringue buttercream, using an electric hand whisk, whisk the egg whites and sugar together in a bowl set over a pan of gently simmering water, until the sugar has dissolved. The egg whites should feel smooth, not gritty.

8 Transfer the hot mixture to the bowl of a stand mixer fitted with a whisk and whisk on medium–high speed to a stiff meringue, then continue whisking until the bowl is completely cool to the touch. Add the butter, little by little, beating continuously to a smooth, fluffy icing. Whisk in the vanilla and honey, then set aside.

9 To make the blueberry compote, tip the blueberries into a pan with the honey and 4 tablespoons of water and bring to the boil over a medium heat. Mix the cornflour with 3 tablespoons of water, add it to the blueberries, and bring back to the boil, stirring gently, so as not to break up the fruit, for 3–4 minutes, until thick and glossy. Remove from the heat and leave to cool.

10 To make the fondant for the pancakes, melt the marshmallows with 2½ tablespoons of water and a small amount of cream food colouring in a large bowl set over a pan of simmering water, stirring continuously.

11 Remove from the heat and, using a wooden spoon, stir in the icing sugar, one quarter at a time, mixing well between each addition, until firm. On a surface greased with vegetable fat, knead the fondant into a ball, then wrap it in cling film and set aside.

12 To assemble the cake, level the sponges then, using a small amount of buttercream, stick one of the sponges onto a serving plate. Spread one third of the buttercream over the sponge and top with a good sprinkling of the crumble and one third of the compote. Top with another sponge.

13 Spread the second sponge with a further one third of the buttercream, another sprinkling of the crumble and one third of the compote, then top with the final sponge.

14 Use the remaining third of the buttercream to cover the top and sides of the cake. Smooth off the excess buttercream with a palette knife to create a crumb coat. Chill for 1 hour, until firm.

Photos overleaf / Continues on page 212

15 Divide the fondant into 12 pieces. On a surface lightly dusted with cornflour, roll ten of the pieces into thin sausages, long enough to wrap around the cake. (Use a piece of string to measure the circumference of the cake and use it as guide when rolling the fondant lengths, if you like.)

16 Wrap one of the fondant lengths around the base of the cake, sticking it together at the ends with edible glue and pinching the join together. Repeat with the remaining nine lengths of fondant until you have ten rolls of fondant around the cake, stacked one on top of the other, resembling a stack of pancakes.

17 Knead the remaining two pieces of fondant together and roll them out to a circle large enough to cover the top of the cake – this is going to be the 'pancake' that tops the stack. Place the circle on top the cake.

18 Combine equal quantities of cream and egg-yellow food colouring and dilute them with 5 tablespoons of vodka (start with small amounts, then add until you get your desired shade – you want it quite a light, cooked-pancake colour at this point). Paint the pancake 'stack' with the colouring.

19 Combine equal quantities of cream, egg-yellow and brown food colouring and dilute the mixture with the remaining 2 tablespoons of vodka, then paint the edges of pancakes to add darker detail, as desired.

20 Spoon the whipped cream over the top of the cake to represent the pancake topping, then sprinkle over another good helping of the crumble and one third of the compote. Dust with icing sugar before serving. (Any leftover granola crumble will keep in an airtight container in the fridge for up to 1 week and is delicious sprinkled over yoghurt or ice cream.)

Nancy made these individual chocolate and orange cakes in Series 5, reinventing a popular classic to create a delicate bake that would look stunning on a cake stand at high tea.

Nancy

Mini Orange Cakes

FOR THE CHOCOLATE PASTE
165g 54% dark chocolate
125g golden syrup
cocoa powder, for dusting

FOR THE JELLY
1 unwaxed orange
60g caster sugar
½ gelatine leaf
2 tsp orange liqueur

FOR THE SPONGE
175g soft baking spread
175g caster sugar
3 large eggs, beaten
1 tsp vanilla extract
175g self-raising flour, sifted
40g milk chocolate,
    broken into pieces

FOR THE ORANGE PASTILLES
4 strips of unwaxed orange peel
    (from the orange for the jelly)
50g caster sugar

FOR THE ORANGE BUTTERCREAM
75g unsalted butter,
    at room temperature
250g icing sugar, sifted

Continues overleaf

1 For the chocolate paste, melt the chocolate in a bowl set over a pan of simmering water until it reaches 40°C/104°F on a sugar thermometer. Melt the golden syrup in a pan over a low heat, until it reaches 40°C/104°F on a sugar thermometer. Remove from the heat. Pour the syrup into the chocolate and stir vigorously until it comes together. Pour into a shallow tray, leave to cool, then chill until firm enough to roll out.

2 For the jelly, using a sharp knife, carefully slice off the top and bottom of the orange. Slice the skin away from the flesh and discard, then remove any remaining white pith. Segment the orange, retaining any juices. Finely chop the segments, again reserving any juice.

3 Place the orange segments and juice in a pan with 3 tablespoons of water and the sugar and bring to the boil. Reduce the heat and simmer for 20 minutes, until reduced. Meanwhile soak the gelatine leaf in a bowl of water until soft.

4 Remove the pan from the heat and blitz the orange syrup with a hand blender until smooth. Add the orange liqueur, then squeeze out the gelatine and stir it into the orange mixture. Transfer to a bowl, leave to cool, then chill to firm up. Once firm, spoon the gel into a medium piping bag fitted with a small plain nozzle and set aside.

5 Heat the oven to 180°C/160°C fan/350°F/Gas 4. For the sponge, whisk the spread and caster sugar together in a stand mixer fitted with the whisk on medium speed for 3–5 minutes, until very light and mousse-like. Add the beaten eggs, a little at a time, and the vanilla extract.

6 Gently fold in the flour, retaining as much air in the mixture as possible. Divide the mixture equally between the mini-sponge holes in the prepared tray and bake for 20 minutes,

Continues overleaf

Mini Orange Cakes *continued*

YOU WILL NEED
sugar thermometer
2 medium piping bags,
   each fitted with a small
   plain nozzle
12-hole mini-sponge tray,
   greased with butter
medium plain nozzle
small piping bag fitted with
   a small writing nozzle
5cm round cutter

until springy to the touch and evenly golden. Cool in the tins for 5 minutes, then transfer to a wire rack to cool completely.

7 For the orange pastilles, bring a small pan of water to the boil. Add the strips of orange peel and boil for 5 minutes. Drain, then using the end of the medium plain nozzle, cut out 12 small circles of peel.

8 Tip the sugar into a small pan with 50ml of water and cook over a low heat, stirring occasionally until the sugar has melted. Add the orange circles, bring to the boil and boil for 5 minutes, until the syrup has thickened. Remove from the heat and transfer the orange circles onto a wire rack and leave to cool, reserving the syrup.

9 For the orange buttercream, beat the butter, icing sugar and 3 tablespoons of the reserved orange syrup (from Step 8) in a stand mixer fitted with the beater – first on low speed, then when the mixture comes together, on high speed for 3–4 minutes, until light and fluffy. Spoon the mixture into the remaining piping bag fitted with a small plain nozzle.

10 To assemble, level the tops of the sponges to make them equal in height, then slice each sponge in half. Pipe the buttercream in small blobs around the edge of the bottom layer of each sponge, then pipe the jelly inside the circle of buttercream. Cover with the sponge tops.

11 To decorate, melt the milk chocolate in a small bowl set over a pan of barely simmering water. Spoon into the small piping bag fitted with a small writing nozzle. Set aside.

12 Roll out the chocolate paste on a surface dusted with cocoa powder to 2mm thick. Using the 5cm round cutter, cut out 12 discs. Paint the tops of the cake with the reserved sugar syrup, then stick on the discs.

13 Pipe two fine lines of milk chocolate across each chocolate disc and decorate each with an orange pastille.

Rhubarb and custard are the perfect combination of tart and sweet, but you could fill the middles of these little vanilla sponges with any rich fruits – just adjust the sugar accordingly.

Rhubarb & Custard Cupcakes

FOR THE RHUBARB FILLING
150g rhubarb, cut into
    large chunks
25g golden caster sugar
finely grated zest of
    ½ unwaxed orange

FOR THE CUPCAKES
100g unsalted butter, softened
100g golden caster sugar
½ tbsp vanilla paste
2 eggs
100g self-raising flour, sifted
15g custard powder
½ tsp baking powder

FOR THE CRUMBLE TOPPING
15g unsalted butter
30g plain flour
a pinch of salt
10g caster sugar
10g light muscovado sugar

FOR THE BUTTERCREAM
125g unsalted butter, softened
250g icing sugar, sifted
½ tsp vanilla paste
20g custard powder
1 tbsp boiling water

YOU WILL NEED
2 baking trays
12-hole muffin tray lined
    with cupcake cases
apple corer
medium disposable piping bag

1 Heat the oven to 180°C/160°C fan/350°F/Gas 4. Spread out the rhubarb on a baking tray and sprinkle with the sugar and orange zest. Cover with foil and bake for 20 minutes, until soft. Cool while you make the cupcakes.

2 Beat the butter, sugar and vanilla in a stand mixer fitted with the beater, on medium speed for 5 minutes, until pale and creamy. Beat in the eggs, one at a time.

3 Mix the flour, custard powder and baking powder together, then add to the mixture, one third at a time, until just combined. Spoon equally into the cupcake cases and bake for 15–20 minutes, until springy and golden. Place the tray on a wire rack for the cakes to cool completely.

4 While the cakes are cooling, blitz the cooled rhubarb and all its juices in a food processor to a smooth purée. Set aside.

5 To make the crumble topping, rub the butter into the flour, until the mixture resembles breadcrumbs. Add the salt and sugars, then spread out the crumble in an even layer on a baking tray. Bake for 10–15 minutes, until golden brown. Set aside to cool.

6 Using an apple corer, cut out a small amount of the centre of each cupcake and fill the hole with 1–2 teaspoons of rhubarb purée, reserving some of the purée for drizzling over the cakes.

7 Make the buttercream. Beat the butter in a stand mixer fitted with the beater, on medium speed for 2–3 minutes, until soft. Add half the icing sugar, then the vanilla and custard powder, and finally the remaining icing sugar and water, beating for 4–5 minutes on medium–high speed, until smooth and fluffy.

8 Spoon the buttercream into the piping bag and cut a 1cm hole in the end. Pipe the buttercream onto the cupcakes in a large dome. Drizzle with the reserved rhubarb purée, and sprinkle with crumble to finish.

SERVES **30**

HANDS-ON **3** HOURS

BAKE **1¼** HOURS

Selasi created the original of this fabulous, tiered cake, decorated with flavoured buttercreams and edible flowers, in Series 7. It makes a formidable celebration cake that can't fail to impress.

Three-tiered Floral Cake

Selasi

FOR THE CARROT SPONGE
450g self-raising flour
2 tsp baking powder
2 tsp ground cinnamon
2 tsp mixed spice
a pinch of salt
380g light muscovado sugar
150g walnuts, chopped
480g carrots, grated
100g desiccated coconut
150g chopped fresh or well-
    drained canned pineapple
6 eggs, beaten
290ml sunflower oil,
    plus extra for greasing

FOR THE LEMON & POPPY SEED SPONGE
250g unsalted butter, softened
250g caster sugar
4 large eggs, beaten
250g self-raising flour, sifted
1 tsp lemon extract
4 tbsp whole milk
4 tbsp poppy seeds

FOR THE VANILLA & STRAWBERRY SPONGE
250g unsalted butter, softened
250g caster sugar
4 eggs, beaten
250g self-raising flour, sifted
1 tsp vanilla essence
4 tbsp whole milk
100g strawberries,
    hulled and chopped

Continues overleaf

1 Heat the oven to 180°C/160°C fan/350°F/Gas 4. Make the carrot sponge. In a large mixing bowl, sift together the flour, baking powder, cinnamon, mixed spice and salt. Stir in the sugar, breaking down any lumps, then the walnuts, carrots, coconut and pineapple. Add the eggs and sunflower oil. Divide the mixture equally between the two 25cm tins and bake for 25–30 minutes, until a skewer inserted into the centres comes out clean. Remove from the oven and cool in the tins.

2 For the lemon and poppy seed sponge, beat the butter and sugar in a stand mixer fitted with the beater, on medium speed for 3–5 minutes, until pale and creamy. Add the eggs, little by little, beating well between each addition. Using a large metal spoon, fold in the flour, lemon extract, milk and poppy seeds. Divide the mixture equally between the two 20cm tins and bake for 20–25 minutes, until a skewer inserted into the centres comes out clean. Remove from the oven and cool in the tins.

3 For the vanilla and strawberry sponge, beat the butter and sugar in a stand mixer fitted with the beater, on medium speed for 3–5 minutes, until pale and creamy. Add the eggs, little by little, beating well between each addition. Using a large metal spoon, fold in the flour, vanilla, milk and strawberries. Divide the mixture equally between the two 15cm tins and bake for 20–25 minutes, or until a skewer inserted into the centres comes out clean. Remove from the oven and cool in the tins.

4 To make the jam, place the raspberries in a small pan and crush them with a fork. Add the sugar, then place over a medium heat and bring to the boil. Boil rapidly for about 10 minutes, until a sugar thermometer reaches 105°C/221°F. Remove from the heat and leave to cool completely.

5 For the lime and mascarpone buttercream, beat the butter and lime zest in a stand mixer fitted with the beater, on medium speed for 3–5 minutes, until fluffy. Gradually add the icing

Continues overleaf

Three-tiered Floral Cake *continued*

FOR THE RASPBERRY JAM
200g raspberries
200g jam sugar

FOR THE LIME & MASCARPONE BUTTERCREAM
200g unsalted butter, softened
juice and finely grated zest
    of 1 unwaxed lime
750g icing sugar, sifted
40g mascarpone
pink food-colouring gel

FOR THE VANILLA CREAM CHEESE BUTTERCREAM
200g unsalted butter, softened
1 tsp vanilla essence
750g icing sugar, sifted
60g full-fat cream cheese
2–3 tbsp semi-skimmed milk
pink food-colouring gel

FOR THE LEMON BUTTERCREAM
120g unsalted butter, softened
finely grated zest of
    1 unwaxed lemon
375g icing sugar
2 tbsp lemon juice
2–3 tbsp semi-skimmed milk
yellow food-colouring gel

TO DECORATE
a selection of edible flowers

YOU WILL NEED
25cm springform tins x 2,
    greased, then base-lined
    with baking paper
20cm springform tins x 2,
    greased, then base-lined
    with baking paper
15cm springform tins x 2,
    greased, then base-lined
    with baking paper
sugar thermometer
30cm round cake drum
3 large piping bags, each fitted
    with a large closed star nozzle
6 cake dowels, 3 cut to the height
    of the large cake and 3 cut
    for the medium cake
20cm cake card
15cm cake card

sugar and beat to combine. Mix in the mascarpone and lime juice, and the pink colouring to the desired dark pink.

6 For the vanilla cream cheese buttercream, beat the butter and vanilla in a stand mixer fitted with the beater, on medium speed for 3–5 minutes. Add the icing sugar and beat until well mixed. Beat in the cream cheese and milk until combined.

7 For the lemon buttercream, beat the butter and lemon zest in a stand mixer fitted with the beater, as before. Gradually add the icing sugar. Beat in the lemon juice, milk, and yellow colouring until the buttercream is your desired shade of yellow.

8 To assemble, spread a little lime buttercream on the cake drum. Sandwich the carrot cakes together with about 4 tablespoons of lime buttercream and place them on the drum. Using a palette knife, spread a crumb coat of buttercream over the top and sides of the stacked cakes.

9 Place the remaining lime buttercream in a piping bag fitted with a star nozzle. Set aside. Position the three longest dowels in a triangle in the middle of the cake, pushing them all the way through so that they touch the cake drum.

10 Spread a little vanilla buttercream on the 20cm cake card. On top, sandwich the lemon poppy-seed cakes with a little of the vanilla buttercream and cover with a crumb coat. Add pink colouring to the remaining vanilla buttercream to create a lighter pink shade. Spoon this into a piping bag and set aside. Position the shorter dowels in the cake in a triangle formation.

11 Spread a little lemon buttercream on the 15cm cake card. On top, stack the vanilla and strawberry cakes using a little jam between each, and use a little lemon buttercream for a crumb coat. Place the remaining lemon buttercream in the remaining piping bag and set aside.

12 Chill all the cakes for 30 minutes to firm up, then stack the poppy-seed cakes on top of the carrot cakes and the vanilla and strawberry cakes on top of the poppy-seed cakes.

13 Pipe rosettes and stars of buttercream all over the cake, using the dark pink icing on the bottom tier, the lighter pink icing on the middle tier and the yellow icing on top. Decorate with edible flowers around each tier and on the top of the cake just before serving.

HOW TO...
ICE A SEMI-NAKED CAKE

In effect, a semi-naked cake is a cake that has been crumb-coated. Naked cakes are bare or un-iced on the side, while a semi-naked cake has a very thin covering of buttercream icing that allows the cake layers to peak through. Use the following instructions for creating semi-naked cakes or for crumb coating cakes you intend to go on to decorate fully.

You will need: cake-decorating turntable (optional) or cake stand or board; palette knife (offset and crank-handled ideally); tall side scraper.

1 Assemble your layer cake as instructed in the recipe, spreading a generous layer of your chosen buttercream between the layers of cake and making sure the layers of sponge are even and flat. Fill and smooth any gaps at the side of the cake, between the layers to give your cake a far more finished and professional look at the end. Once you have a smooth surface, you're ready for the semi-naked coating.

2 Generously spread some additional buttercream around the sides of the cake with a palette knife using gentle pressure and with one hand on top of the cake to secure it. Occasionally, revolve the turntable or cake plate or board while you work around the cake, to make sure it is evenly coated.

3 Once you have covered the side in a single coating of buttercream, spread an even layer over the top of the cake, spreading it out with the palette knife.

4 Once the whole cake is covered, use a side scraper to smooth off any excess covering on the sides, spreading and removing the buttercream until you are happy with the finish and coverage – expose some areas of the cake and leave others more covered.

5 Put the cake in the fridge to chill and firm up for at least 30 minutes to 1 hour. If chilling for more than 2 hours, cover loosely with cling film after the first hour.

SEMI-NAKED CAKE DECORATING TIPS:

» Bake the cake as close to decorating as possible so the sponge is fresh. Leave it to cool before decorating.

» To keep the sponge cake moist and prevent it drying out, brush the cake with a simple sugar syrup. You could add coffee or even a liqueur to the syrup to add extra flavour to your cake.

» Make sure the buttercream is the right consistency for spreading; it should have a light, fluffy, whippy texture.

» There may be a little buttercream crown around the top edge of your cake after you've smoothed the sides. Using the palette knife, smooth the buttercream crown inwards, towards the middle of the cake, aiming to create sharp edges and a completely level top.

In Series 8, Sophie made this simple, tropical-tasting sandwich cake, topped with a pineapple flower made with baked pineapple 'leather'.

Sophie

Pineapple & Coconut Sandwich Cake

FOR THE SPONGE
1 pineapple, peeled, cut into
    3 x 5mm-thick rounds, then
    the remainder cored and
    cut into small chunks
170g unsalted butter, softened
225g caster sugar
5 large eggs, beaten
240g self-raising flour, sifted
100g fresh coconut chunks,
    peeled and blitzed to a gravel
15g coconut flakes, toasted,
    to decorate

**FOR THE COCONUT
MERINGUE BUTTERCREAM**
300g caster sugar
3 egg whites
250g unsalted butter,
    diced and softened
½ tsp coconut flavouring,
    plus extra to taste,
    if necessary

YOU WILL NEED
20cm sandwich tins x 2,
    greased, then base-lined
    with baking paper
baking sheet lined with
    baking paper
mini-muffin tray
sugar thermometer
large piping bag fitted with
    a medium plain nozzle

1 Heat the oven to 180°C/160°C fan/350°F/Gas 4.

2 Weigh out 150g of the pineapple chunks for the cake mixture, drain thoroughly and pat dry with kitchen paper. Set aside 50g for decoration (eat the rest).

3 Beat the butter and sugar in a stand mixer fitted with the beater, on medium speed for 3–5 minutes, until pale and creamy. Gradually add the eggs, little by little, beating well after each addition. Add 1 tablespoon of the flour with the last three additions of egg, then sift in the remaining flour and fold to combine. Mix in the coconut 'gravel' and pineapple chunks.

4 Divide the mixture equally between the prepared tins. Bake for about 25–30 minutes, until a skewer inserted into the centres comes out clean. Cool in the tins for 2 minutes, then turn out onto a wire rack to cool completely. Reduce the oven to 140°C/120°C fan/275°F/Gas 1.

5 Prepare the pineapple flower. Put the 3 pineapple slices on the lined baking sheet. Bake for 15–20 minutes, then turn over and bake for a further 15–20 minutes, until they are dry but flexible, with golden edges. Press each slice into a hole in the muffin tray. Return to the oven for a further 20 minutes or so, until dry and golden. Cool in the tray, then stack the slices into each other to make a flower. Set aside.

6 Make the buttercream. Dissolve the sugar in 90ml of water in a medium pan over a low heat (about 3–5 minutes).

7 While the sugar is dissolving, whisk the egg whites in a stand mixer fitted with the whisk to soft peaks. Once the sugar has completely dissolved, increase the heat to a rapid boil until the syrup reaches 121°C/250°F on a sugar thermometer. Remove the pan from the heat.

Continues overleaf

Fruit & Nut **227**

8 With the whisk at full speed, pour the hot syrup onto the egg whites in a thin stream. Continue whisking until the meringue is very thick and glossy and has cooled to room temperature.

9 Gradually add the butter, whisking after each addition until the buttercream is smooth and thick. Incorporate the coconut flavouring, adding more to taste, if you prefer. Cover the bowl and chill until firm enough to pipe.

10 To assemble, place one sponge, top-side down, on a cake stand. Spoon the buttercream into the large piping bag fitted with the plain nozzle. Pipe large 'kisses' on top of the sponge, saving half the buttercream for the next layer. Top with the second sponge, top-side upwards, and pipe more kisses.

11 Place the pineapple flower in the centre of the cake and decorate with toasted coconut flakes and the reserved 50g of pineapple, chopped into 1cm pieces.

CHAPTER FIVE

Free-from

A classic cake adapted for vegan taste buds – see the table over the page for the quantities to make the cake in alternative sizes.

Vegan Lemon Drizzle

FOR THE SPONGE
150ml soya milk
1 tbsp apple cider vinegar
1 tsp baking powder
100g self-raising flour, sifted
150g ground almonds
90g solid vegetable fat
110g golden caster sugar
1 tsp vanilla paste
finely grated zest of
    1 unwaxed lemon
berries or edible flowers,
    to decorate (optional)

FOR THE DRIZZLE
juice of 1 lemon
2 tbsp caster sugar

FOR THE LEMON ICING
250g fondant icing sugar, sifted
juice of ½ lemon

YOU WILL NEED
450g loaf tin, greased,
    then lined (base and sides)
    with baking paper
cocktail stick

1 Heat the oven to 180°C/160°C fan/350°F/Gas 4.

2 Put the soya milk in a jug and add the vinegar. Leave for 5 minutes to curdle slightly. In a bowl stir together the baking powder, flour and ground almonds.

3 Beat the fat, sugar, vanilla and lemon zest in a stand mixer fitted with the beater, on a medium speed for 3–4 minutes, until pale and creamy.

4 With the mixer on a low speed, gradually add the curdled soya milk and beat for 30–60 seconds, until combined. Add the flour mixture, and mix on low until just incorporated.

5 Spoon the cake mixture into the loaf tin and bake it for 1 hour, until the top is golden and a skewer inserted into the centre comes out clean. Set aside in the tin to cool a little, while you make the drizzle.

6 Mix together the lemon juice and sugar in a small jug, until the sugar has dissolved. Pierce the still-warm cake all over with the cocktail stick and pour the drizzle over the top. Set aside in the tin and leave to cool completely.

7 To make the lemon icing, put the icing sugar in a jug. Add the lemon juice, a little at a time, until you have a very thick, but pourable icing. (You may not need all the juice.)

8 Once the cake has cooled, remove it from the tin and place it on a serving plate or stand. Using a spoon, drizzle or pour the icing over the top of the cake, allowing it to drip off the edges. Serve as it is, or decorate with berries or edible flowers (violas are lovely), if you wish.

SCALING QUANTITIES
VEGAN LEMON DRIZZLE CAKE

Use these quantities to adapt the recipe on the previous page for a 5cm-deep, round 20cm, 25cm or 30cm cake tin, a larger loaf and a traybake.

	20cm round, deep cake tin	25cm round, deep cake tin	30cm round, deep cake tin	900g loaf tin	23 x 30cm traybake tin
For the sponge					
soya milk	300ml	460g	675g	300ml	365g
apple cider vinegar	2 tbsp	3 tbsp	4½ tbsp	2 tbsp	2½ tbsp
self-raising flour, sifted	200g	315g	450g	200g	390g
ground almonds	300g	450g	600g	300g	525g
baking powder	2 tsp	3 tsp	1 tbsp + 1 tsp	2 tsp	2½ tsp
golden caster sugar	220g	350g	500g	220g	425g
solid vegetable fat	180g	280g	400g	180g	340g
vanilla paste	2 tsp	2½ tsp	1 tbsp	2 tsp	2 tsp
finely grated zest of...	2 lemons	3 lemons	4 lemons	2 lemons	3 lemons
For the drizzle					
juice of...	2 lemons	3 lemons	4 lemons	2 lemons	3 lemons
caster sugar	2 tbsp	3 tbsp	4 tbsp	2 tbsp	3 tbsp
For the lemon icing					
fondant icing sugar, sifted	200g	300g	400g	125g	300g
juice of...	1 lemon	1½ lemons	2 lemons	½ lemon	1½ lemons
Baking time @ 180°C/ 160°C fan/350°F/Gas 4	1 hour	1 hour– 1 hour 10 mins	1 hour 15 mins	1 hour	45 mins

SERVES	HANDS-ON	BAKE
20	**2** HOURS	**2** HOURS

Suitable for vegans and delicious for everyone, this celebration cake was Briony's creation during Series 9. Aquafaba is the water from a can of chickpeas and behaves just like egg white.

Dairy-free Hazelnut Mocha Cake

Briony

FOR THE SPONGE
565g self-raising flour, sifted
600g golden caster sugar
125g cacao powder
1½ tsp baking powder
1½ tsp salt
200g roasted hazelnuts, chopped
200ml dairy-free spread, melted
400ml soya coffee & hazelnut milk
250ml walnut oil
1 tsp xanthan gum
3½ tbsp espresso-strength instant coffee
50ml boiling water

FOR THE MERINGUE KISSES
75ml aquafaba
100g caster sugar
1 tsp xanthan gum
edible gold lustre powder

FOR THE GANACHE
300g vegan dark chocolate, broken into pieces
300g full-fat coconut cream
a pinch of salt
2 tbsp coffee liqueur

FOR THE TRUFFLES
130g vegan chocolate buttons
45g full-fat coconut cream
50g chopped roasted hazelnuts

Continues overleaf

1 Heat the oven to 180°C/160°C fan/350°F/Gas 4.

2 Make the sponge. In a large bowl, stir together the flour, sugar, cacao, baking powder, salt and hazelnuts.

3 In a medium bowl, using a balloon whisk, combine the melted spread, soya coffee and hazelnut milk, walnut oil and xanthan gum. Dissolve the coffee in the boiling water, then whisk it into the bowl with the other wet ingredients.

4 Combine the wet and dry ingredients until smooth, then divide the batter equally mixture the three prepared tins. Bake for 30–35 minutes, until just firm and a skewer inserted into the centres comes out clean. Cool in the tins for 5 minutes, then turn out onto a wire rack to cool completely.

5 Make the meringues. Reduce the oven temperature to 110°C/90°C fan/225°F/Gas ½. Whisk the aquafaba in the bowl of a stand mixer fitted with the whisk, on high speed for about 5 minutes, until doubled in size and thick and foamy.

6 With the whisk on a low speed, add the caster sugar and xanthan gum, then increase the speed to maximum and whisk for about 10 minutes, until the mixture forms stiff peaks.

7 Place the meringue in the large piping bag fitted with a large star nozzle. Pipe 'kisses' over the baking trays (you'll have more meringue than you need – you can freeze the spares once baked; or keep them in an airtight container for up to 1 week). Bake the meringues for 90 minutes, until dried out. Allow to cool, then dust with gold lustre powder.

8 Meanwhile, make the ganache. Place the chocolate in a heatproof bowl. Warm the coconut cream and salt in a pan

Continues overleaf

FOR THE RASPBERRY JAM
250g raspberries
250g jam sugar
juice of ½ lemon

FOR THE ICING
50g dairy-free spread
150g icing sugar, sifted
½ tsp vanilla extract
green food-colouring paste
red food-colouring paste

TO FINISH
2 tbsp freeze-dried raspberries
100g raspberries

YOU WILL NEED
23cm sandwich tins x 3,
    greased, then base-lined
    with baking paper
large piping bag fitted with
    a large closed star nozzle
2 baking trays lined with
    baking paper
8cm square, shallow container
melon baller
sugar thermometer
small piping bag fitted with
    a small closed star nozzle
medium piping bag fitted with
    a large closed star nozzle
icing scraper

over a low heat until starting to bubble around the edge. Pour the coconut cream over the chocolate, leave for 5 minutes, then mix until smooth. Stir in the coffee liqueur. Cover with cling film and chill for about 2 hours, until set.

9 Make the truffles. Place the chocolate buttons in a heatproof bowl. Warm the coconut cream in a pan over a low heat until starting to bubble around the edge. Pour the coconut cream over the chocolate, leave for 5 minutes, then mix until smooth. Pour into the square container and chill to set.

10 Put the chopped hazelnuts in a small bowl. When truffle mixture has hardened, use the melon baller to scoop up 10 balls. Roll each ball in the hazelnuts to coat, then chill to set.

11 Make the jam. Cook the raspberries in a small pan over a medium heat for 5 minutes, or until soft and pulpy. Reduce the heat to low, add the sugar and lemon juice and heat gently until the sugar has dissolved. Increase the heat and simmer for about 5 minutes, or until jam reaches 105°C/221°F on the sugar thermometer. Transfer to a bowl and chill until needed.

12 Make the icing. Whisk the spread by hand until light and fluffy. Sift in half the icing sugar and whisk to combine, then add the vanilla and remaining icing sugar and whisk again.

13 Put 2 tablespoons of the icing in a small bowl and add green food colouring until leaf-green. Place in the small piping bag fitted with the small star nozzle. Colour the remaining icing red and place in the medium piping bag fitted with the large star nozzle. Set both aside.

14 Whisk the cooled ganache in a stand mixer on medium speed until light and fluffy.

15 To assemble, cover the bottom sponge with a thin layer of ganache, then a thin layer of jam. Repeat for the next layer, then place the last sponge, top downwards, on top. Spread the remaining ganache over the top and side of the layered cakes, then use an icing scraper to smooth the icing around the sides.

16 Pipe 3 or 4 large rosettes of red icing to make roses and use the green icing to pipe small rosettes representing leaves for each rose. Scatter dried raspberries over the cake and decorate as you wish with truffles, meringues and fresh raspberries.

You can make the honeycomb for these cupcakes in advance, if you like – it will last for up to a week if it is well wrapped.

Dairy-free Caramel Cupcakes

FOR THE CUPCAKES
125g light muscovado sugar
125g dairy-free spread
½ tsp vanilla paste
2 eggs
2 tbsp dairy-free milk
125g self-raising flour, sifted
½ tsp baking powder

FOR THE CARAMEL
90g light muscovado sugar
150ml oat cream
25g dairy-free spread
½ tsp salt

FOR THE HONEYCOMB
100g caster sugar
35g runny honey
1 tsp bicarbonate of soda

FOR THE BUTTERCREAM
100g dairy-free spread
200g icing sugar, sifted
1 tsp vanilla paste
1 tbsp caramel (optional)
1 tsp hot water, if necessary

YOU WILL NEED
12-hole muffin tray lined
    with 12 cupcake cases
20cm-square baking dish
    lined with baking paper
apple corer
large piping bag fitted with
    a medium plain nozzle

1 Heat the oven to 180°C/160°C fan/350°F/Gas 4.

2 Beat all the cupcake ingredients together in a stand mixer fitted with the beater, on medium speed for 3–4 minutes, until smooth and combined.

3 Spoon the mixture into the cupcake cases and bake for 15–20 minutes, until golden brown and just firm to the touch. Remove the cupcakes from the tray and place them on a wire rack to cool.

4 Place all the caramel ingredients in a small pan over a medium heat. Bring to the boil and boil for 5–10 minutes, until reduced by half to a thick caramel. Pour into a bowl and cool for 10–15 minutes, then chill for 1 hour.

5 While the caramel chills, make the honeycomb. Heat the sugar and honey in a medium pan over a low heat for 5 minutes, until the sugar has dissolved, then turn up the heat and boil for about 4–5 minutes, until the mixture turns a golden caramel colour. Remove from the heat and immediately whisk in the bicarbonate of soda, taking care as the mixture will immediately foam up. Pour into the prepared baking dish and leave it to set for 30–45 minutes.

6 Meanwhile, make the buttercream. Beat the spread, sugar and vanilla in a small bowl with an electric hand whisk until smooth and creamy. Add 1 tablespoon of the caramel, if you wish, and stir through to combine.

7 Using an apple corer, remove the middle of each cupcake and fill each cavity with caramel.

8 Fill the piping bag with the buttercream. Pipe around the edge of each cupcake, working inwards in a spiral to cover the tops in a thick layer. Smash the honeycomb into chunks and arrange over the cupcakes.

Try to leave a few hours for this cheesecake to chill in the fridge before serving – it will help to really bring out the flavour in every layer.

Gluten-free Berry Cheesecake

FOR THE BISCUITS
100g dairy-free spread
60g light muscovado sugar
1 tsp vanilla paste
200g gluten-free plain
flour, sifted
30g gluten-free rolled oats
30g desiccated coconut
a pinch of salt

FOR THE CHEESECAKE
150g dairy-free spread
1 quantity of gluten- and
dairy-free biscuits (above)
800g dairy-free cream cheese
180g coconut yogurt
200g golden caster sugar
1 tsp vanilla paste
3 eggs, beaten

FOR THE BERRY COMPOTE
1 tsp cornflour
250g frozen blueberries
250g frozen strawberries

YOU WILL NEED
large baking tray, greased,
then base-lined with
baking paper
23cm springform tin,
greased, then base-lined
with baking paper

1 Heat the oven to 200°C/180°C fan/400°F/Gas 6.

2 Make the biscuits. Mix the spread and sugar together in a bowl with a wooden spoon. Stir in the vanilla and 2 tablespoons of water.

3 In a separate bowl, combine the remaining ingredients. Add them to the first bowl and bring together to a smooth dough. Roll out the dough on a lightly floured surface to about 5mm thick and cut into similar-sized pieces. (You don't need to be precise.) Transfer to the prepared baking tray.

4 Bake for 15–20 minutes, until golden. Remove from the oven, then transfer to a wire rack to cool. Once cool, place the biscuits in a freezer bag and bash with a rolling pin to a crumb.

5 Make the cheesecake. Beat the dairy-free spread in a large bowl to soften. Stir in the biscuit crumbs and tip into the tin. Press down evenly with the back of a spoon and chill the base for 15–20 minutes to firm up.

6 Meanwhile, make the filling. Heat the oven to 200°C/180°C fan/400°F/Gas 6. Beat together the dairy-free cream cheese and coconut yogurt with a wooden spoon, until smooth. Add the sugar and mix until dissolved. Add the vanilla, then add the eggs, a little at a time, beating well between each addition. Pour the mixture over the base, and bake for 1–1¼ hours, until golden. Set aside to cool (it may sink a little – that's okay).

7 Make the compote. Mix the cornflour with 2 tablespoons of water to a paste. Put the blueberries and strawberries in a medium pan over a low heat for 2–3 minutes, and bring to a simmer. Add the cornflour mixture and mix well.

8 Increase the heat and bring to the boil, then reduce the heat and simmer for 2–3 minutes, until the fruit has softened, but is still intact. Set aside to cool completely, then spoon onto the cheesecake. Chill for at least 2 hours before serving.

You could top this cake with a drizzle of fruit juice or maple syrup. Soak the fruit overnight, if you have time, to give the best results.

Coconut Sugar Fruitcake

100g glacé cherries
125g sultanas
125g raisins
350ml medium-strength
   hot, black tea
270g self-raising flour, sifted
200g coconut sugar
½ tsp ground ginger
1 tsp mixed spice
2 eggs

YOU WILL NEED
900g loaf tin, greased,
   then lined (base and sides)
   with baking paper

1 Place the cherries, sultanas and raisins in a bowl and pour over the hot tea. Set aside covered with cling film and leave the fruit to soak for 6–8 hours, or ideally overnight.

2 Heat oven to 180°C/160°C fan/350°F/Gas 4.

3 Put the flour, coconut sugar, ginger and mixed spice in a large mixing bowl and stir to combine. Add the eggs and the soaked fruit (including any remaining soaking liquid) and mix until well combined.

4 Spoon the mixture into the prepared tin and bake for 1 hour, until a skewer inserted into the centre comes out pasty (but not wet).

5 Leave the loaf to cool in the tin for 10–15 minutes, then transfer it to a wire rack to cool completely before slicing.

Once you master the ombre technique, you can turn any cake into a showstopper. Use any leftover buttercream to decorate fairy cakes, and bake the sponges in batches if you don't have five tins.

Gluten-free Lemon Ombre Cake

FOR THE SPONGE
500g unsalted butter, softened
500g golden caster sugar
finely grated zest of
    2 unwaxed lemons
1 tsp vanilla paste
12 eggs, beaten
500g gluten-free self-raising
    flour, sifted
1 tsp gluten-free baking powder

FOR THE DRIZZLE
juice of 3 lemons
150g caster sugar

FOR THE BUTTERCREAM
1.2kg unsalted butter, softened
finely grated zest of
    4 unwaxed lemons
3 tsp vanilla paste
2.4kg icing sugar, sifted
yellow food-colouring paste

YOU WILL NEED
20cm sandwich tins x 5,
    greased, then lined
    (base and sides)
    with baking paper
20cm round cake drum
25cm round cake drum
cake-decorating turntable
large crank-handled
    palette knife
5 large disposable piping bags
tall side scraper

1 Heat the oven to 200°C/180°C fan/400°F/Gas 6.

2 Beat the butter, sugar, zest and vanilla in a stand mixer fitted with the beater, on medium speed for 1–2 minutes, until pale and creamy. Add the eggs, little by little, beating well between each addition.

3 Add the flour and baking powder, one third at a time, mixing on a low speed until incorporated.

4 Divide the mixture between the five tins and bake for 20–25 minutes, until springy to the touch and a skewer inserted into the centres comes out clean. Remove from the oven and leave to cool in the tins for 5 minutes, then turn out onto wire racks to cool completely.

5 While the cakes are baking, make the drizzle. Put the lemon juice and sugar in a pan with 50ml of water, and place over a medium heat for 2–3 minutes, stirring occasionally, until the sugar has dissolved. Remove from the heat, leave to cool, then brush a little drizzle over the sponges on the racks.

6 Make the buttercream. Beat the butter, zest and vanilla in a stand mixer fitted with the beater, on a medium speed for 1 minute, until fluffy. Add the icing sugar, one quarter at a time, starting on a low speed, then increasing to high for 1 minute between each addition. Set aside.

7 Level the sponges and brush with a little more drizzle. Put a little buttercream on the 20cm cake drum and top with the first sponge. Put the cake on the 25cm drum, then on the turntable. Spread a tenth of the buttercream over the top of the cake, and over the edges a little.

8 Top with another sponge and repeat with another layer of buttercream. Repeat with a further two sponges, then top with the final sponge, placing it cut-side downwards.

Continues overleaf

9 Spread one tenth of the remaining buttercream all around the sides of the cake to create a crumb coat. Use a further tenth of the buttercream to spread a thin, even layer over the top of the cake.

10 Using the palette knife, smooth off the excess covering until the sides are smooth and neat. Remove the cake from the turntable and chill for 1 hour.

11 For the ombre layer, divide the remaining buttercream into five separate bowls. Using the yellow food colouring, tint the buttercream in four of the bowls a different shade of yellow, from bright to pale. Place each shade (including the plain) into a disposable piping bag. Place the cake back on the turntable.

12 Snip a 1cm hole in the end of each piping bag. Starting with the brightest shade of yellow, pipe in circles around the bottom of the cake, making two or three rings up the side of the cake, so that you cover about a fifth of the height of the cake.

13 Repeat for the remaining shades, getting lighter each time, then use the plain buttercream just for the uppermost edge and the top of the cake, piping around the top edge and roughly filling in the top surface of the cake. Using the palette knife, smooth the buttercream over the top of the cake.

14 Using a tall side scraper, swoop all around the cake to create an ombre effect. Hold the scraper edge against the cake, with the flat side of the scraper at a 45° angle to the side of the cake. In one, confident motion, spin the turntable while sweeping the buttercream. Once you get back to your starting point, remove the scraper in a swift motion.

15 Using a sharp knife, gently remove any excess buttercream that has popped up on top of the cake. If you need or want to neaten your finish, go round once (but only once) more with a clean scraper. Place the cake back in the fridge to firm up.

16 To serve, use a palette knife to lift the whole cake off the 25cm drum and onto a cake stand or serving plate.

MAKES
16

HANDS-ON
20 MINS

BAKE
30 MINS

These gluten-free brownies are made with ground almonds in place of flour. Keep the raspberries whole when adding them to the mixture to create juicy pockets of deliciousness.

Gluten-free Chocolate Berry Brownies

260g 70% dark chocolate,
  broken into pieces
130g unsalted butter, diced
1 tsp vanilla paste
260g light muscovado sugar
4 eggs, beaten
60g cocoa powder
260g ground almonds
150g raspberries
30g flaked almonds

YOU WILL NEED
22cm square cake tin, greased
  and lined (base and sides)
  with baking paper

1 Heat the oven to 200°C/180°C fan/400°F/Gas 6.

2 Melt the chocolate, butter, vanilla and sugar in a bowl set over a pan of simmering water, stirring occasionally, for 5 minutes. Remove the bowl from the pan, add the eggs and stir until fully incorporated.

3 Using a metal spoon, gently fold in the cocoa powder and ground almonds, then carefully mix in the raspberries – be gentle so as not to squash them.

4 Pour the brownie mixture into the prepared tin and sprinkle over the flaked almonds.

5 Bake the brownie mixture for about 30 minutes, until a skewer inserted into the centre comes out pasty (but not wet). Leave the brownie to cool completely in the tin before slicing into 16 squares.

The blush pink rhubarb in the almond-rich polenta sponge looks stunning, and this fruity cake is immensely comforting – like a hug in a cake.

Gluten-free Rhubarb & Polenta Cake

200g caster sugar
150g unsalted butter, softened
1 tsp vanilla paste
finely grated zest of
    1 unwaxed orange
3 eggs, beaten
150g polenta
1½ tsp gluten-free
    baking powder
100g ground almonds
400g forced rhubarb, trimmed
    and thickly sliced
flaked almonds, to decorate
icing sugar, for dusting

YOU WILL NEED
20cm round, deep, loose-
    bottomed cake tin, greased,
    then lined (base and sides)
    with baking paper

1 Heat the oven to 180°C/160°C fan/350°F/Gas 4.

2 Beat the sugar, butter and vanilla in a stand mixer fitted with the beater, on medium speed for 2–3 minutes, until pale and creamy. Reduce the speed to low, then add the orange zest. Add the eggs, little by little, beating well between each addition, until combined.

3 Fold in the polenta, baking powder and ground almonds, mixing to a dropping consistency. Spoon half the mixture over the base of the prepared tin. Level with a palette knife.

4 Reserve a few pieces of rhubarb for decoration, then arrange the remaining rhubarb over the cake mixture in the tin. Top with the remaining mixture, spreading it out evenly, and decorate with the reserved rhubarb pieces.

5 Bake the sponge for 1–1¼ hours, until well risen and golden and a skewer inserted into the centre comes out clean. Leave to cool for 1–2 hours, then turn out and place the cake top-side upwards on a cake plate. Scatter over a few flaked almonds and dust with icing sugar, to decorate.

The 'doneness' test for these cupcakes is slightly different to other cakes: when inserted, the skewer should come out sticky, with some cake mixture on it, to make sure the finished texture is fudgy.

Vegan Chocolate Fudge Cupcakes

FOR THE CUPCAKES
175ml soya milk
1 tsp apple cider vinegar
    or lemon juice
200g light muscovado sugar
125ml sunflower oil
1 tsp vanilla extract or paste
175g self-raising flour, sifted
65g cocoa powder
½ tsp baking powder
½ tsp bicarbonate of soda
¼ tsp salt
200g coconut yogurt

FOR THE CHOCOLATE ICING
90g good-quality, 70% dairy-
    free dark chocolate, broken
    into pieces, plus optional 50g
    (grated), for decorating
40g oat or coconut cream
90g dairy-free spread
1 tsp vanilla paste
250g icing sugar, sifted

YOU WILL NEED
12-hole muffin tray, lined
    with 12 cupcake cases

1 Heat the oven to 200°C/180°C fan/400°F/Gas 6.

2 Put the soya milk in a jug and add the vinegar. Leave for 5 minutes to curdle slightly.

3 Whisk together the sugar, oil and vanilla in a bowl. In a separate, large bowl, mix together the flour, cocoa powder, baking powder, bicarbonate of soda and salt.

4 Using a balloon whisk, gradually incorporate the soya milk mixture and the sugar mixture into the bowl with the dry ingredients, then add the coconut yogurt and mix until smooth and just incorporated.

5 Spoon the cupcake mixture equally into the cupcake cases. Bake for 20 minutes, until a skewer inserted into the centres comes out pasty (but not wet). Leave to cool in the tin for 30 minutes, then transfer to a wire rack to cool completely.

6 To make the icing, melt the chocolate in the dairy-free cream in a bowl set over a pan of simmering water. Once the chocolate has melted (about 3–4 minutes), stir to combine, then remove from the heat and leave to cool slightly.

7 Beat the spread, vanilla and icing sugar in a stand mixer fitted with the beater, on medium speed for 1–2 minutes, until fluffy. Add the chocolate mixture and beat on a low speed for 1 minute, until smooth.

8 To decorate, load a mound of buttercream onto the top of each cake. Spread evenly with the swirl of the knife, then finish with a sprinkling of grated dark chocolate, if you wish.

Coconut sugar and naturally sweet carrots and cinnamon, along with a cream cheese and maple topping, give this cake sweetness without the need for refined white sugar.

Naturally Sweet Carrot & Walnut Cake

FOR THE SPONGE
3 eggs
250g coconut sugar
100ml vegetable oil
150g plain flour, sifted
1 tsp baking powder
1 tsp ground cinnamon
1 tsp mixed spice
300g grated carrot
50g walnut pieces

FOR THE TOPPING
250g full-fat cream cheese
2–3 tbsp maple syrup
broken-up walnut halves
    and a few edible flowers,
    to decorate

YOU WILL NEED
20cm round, deep cake
    tin, greased, then lined
    (base and sides) with
    baking paper

1 Heat the oven to 200°C/180°C fan/400°F/Gas 6.

2 Make the sponge. Whisk together the eggs, coconut sugar and vegetable oil in a bowl. In a separate, large bowl, mix together the flour, baking powder and spices, then stir through the carrot and walnuts until evenly distributed.

3 Add the wet ingredients to the dry and use a wooden spoon to gently combine.

4 Pour the mixture into the prepared tin and bake for 25–30 minutes, until a skewer inserted into the centre comes out clean. Leave to cool in the tin for 5 minutes, then turn out onto a wire rack to cool completely.

5 To make the topping, put the cream cheese in a bowl and add 2 tablespoons of the maple syrup. Stir to combine, then taste, and add a little more maple syrup, if needed. Mix until smooth and silky.

6 Level the cooled cake with a bread knife, then transfer it to a cake plate. Using a palette knife, spread the topping evenly over the cake, making swirls for texture, if you wish.

7 Sprinkle the walnut pieces in a ring around the edge of the topping, and dot with edible flowers for a little colour.

A little goes a long way with this intensely delicious and multi-textured traybake – it is the perfect accompaniment to a cup of tea or coffee.

Chocolate & Nougat Layer Cake

FOR THE SPONGE
2 tsp instant espresso powder
150ml hot water
200g gluten-free plain
   flour, sifted
200g caster sugar
75g cocoa, sifted
2 tsp bicarbonate of soda
1 tsp baking powder
½ tsp salt
2 large eggs
150g buttermilk
150ml vegetable oil
1 tbsp vanilla extract

FOR THE NOUGAT
60g unsalted butter
200g caster sugar
4 tbsp evaporated milk
213g tub of marshmallow
   cream spread
65g peanut butter
1 tsp vanilla extract
190g salted peanuts,
   roughly chopped

FOR THE CARAMEL
150g dulce de leche
sprinkling of crushed sea salt

FOR THE CHOCOLATE
250g 54% dark chocolate,
   finely chopped
125g double cream
25g salted peanuts,
   roughly chopped

YOU WILL NEED
30 x 23cm traybake tin, greased,
   then lined (base and sides)
   with baking paper

1 Heat the oven to 180°C/160°C fan/350°F/Gas 4. Dissolve the espresso powder in the hot water and leave to cool.

2 For the sponge, beat the flour, sugar, cocoa, bicarbonate of soda, baking powder, salt, eggs, buttermilk, oil, vanilla and cooled coffee in a stand mixer fitted with the beater, on medium speed for 2 minutes, until smooth.

3 Pour the mixture into the prepared tin and bake for 20 minutes, until firm and a skewer inserted into the centre comes out clean. Leave to cool in the tin. (The sponge may be domed at first but it will fall and flatten when cooled.)

4 For the nougat, melt the butter in a medium pan over a medium heat. Add the sugar and evaporated milk, stirring until dissolved, then bring to the boil. Reduce the heat and simmer for 5 minutes, stirring occasionally until golden brown. Remove the pan from heat and pour the mixture into a stand mixer fitted with the beater. Leave to cool for 5 minutes.

5 Add the marshmallow cream spread, peanut butter and vanilla extract to the bowl and beat on a low speed for 1 minute, until well combined, then fold in the peanuts.

6 Spread the dulce de leche over the cooled sponge and sprinkle sparingly with sea salt. Pour the warm nougat over the cake and smooth with a palette knife. Leave to set for 1 hour.

7 For the chocolate layer, place the chopped chocolate in a bowl. Pour the cream into a small pan and place over a medium heat. As soon as it comes to the boil, pour it over the chocolate and leave to stand for 1 minute, then stir until smooth. Leave to cool slightly, then pour the mixture over the nougat layer and sprinkle with chopped peanuts. Chill for 2–3 hours, until set, then turn out and cut into 24 slices.

You can make this cake more or less marbled simply by swirling the mixtures together more or less with the skewer – the more you swirl, the more patterns you'll create.

Vegan Marble Cake

300ml soya milk
1 tbsp apple cider vinegar
    or lemon juice
220g golden caster sugar
175g dairy-free spread
2 tsp vanilla paste
325g self-raising flour, sifted
1 tsp baking powder
3 tbsp cocoa powder

YOU WILL NEED
2 medium disposable
    piping bags
25cm round bundt tin, greased

1 Heat the oven to 200°C/180°C fan/400°F/Gas 6.

2 Put the soya milk in a jug and stir in the vinegar or lemon juice. Leave for 5 minutes to curdle slightly.

3 Beat the sugar, spread and vanilla in a stand mixer fitted with the beater, on high speed for 2–3 minutes, until pale and creamy.

4 With the mixer on a low speed, gradually add the curdled soya milk and beat for 30–60 seconds. Add the flour and baking powder, and mix on low until just incorporated.

5 Spoon one-third of the mixture into a separate bowl and add the cocoa powder. Then, spoon the chocolate mixture into a medium piping bag.

6 Spoon the vanilla mixture into a separate piping bag, snip a 2cm opening in the end and pipe one third into the greased bundt tin, in a random pattern.

7 Snip the end of the piping bag containing the chocolate mixture and randomly dot blobs of chocolate in and around the vanilla. Then, switch back – alternating bag by bag until you have used up both mixtures.

8 To marble the sponge, drag a skewer through the mixtures in a wavy motion all around the tin, so you can see streaks.

9 Bake the sponge for 25 minutes, until a skewer inserted into the ring comes out clean. Allow to cool in the tin for 5–10 minutes, then turn out onto a wire rack to cool completely.

Kim-Joy's vegan celebration cake from Series 9 requires a bit of skill, but is sure to impress. If you don't have time for the whole creation, try making just the biscuits to enjoy with a cup of tea.

Vegan Lavender & Lemon Fox Cake

Kim-Joy

FOR THE 23CM BASE TIER
675g extra-fine self-raising sponge flour, sifted
410g caster sugar
5 tsp edible lavender
2¼ tsp baking powder
1 tsp salt
635g soya milk
230g sunflower oil
5 tsp aquafaba
2½ tsp white wine vinegar

FOR THE 18CM TOP TIER
435g extra-fine self-raising sponge flour, sifted
260g caster sugar
1½ tsp baking powder
¾ tsp salt
2 tsp edible dried lavender
400g soya milk
150g sunflower oil
4½ tsp aquafaba
3 tsp white wine vinegar

FOR THE VEGAN LEMON CURD
35g cornflour
100g lemon-infused sugar
juice of 5 lemons
75g soya milk
85g extra-virgin coconut oil

FOR THE VEGAN BISCUITS
150g plain flour, sifted
a pinch of salt
20g caster sugar
½ tsp vanilla paste
80g coconut oil

Continues overleaf

1 Heat the oven to 180°C/160°C fan/350°F/Gas 4. Make the sponge for the bottom tier. Mix all the dry ingredients together in a large bowl and whisk all the wet ingredients together in another large bowl. Add the dry ingredients into the wet, and whisk until smooth and just combined.

2 Pour the mixture equally into the three larger tins and bake for 15–20 minutes, until a skewer inserted in the centres comes out clean. Immediately turn out the sponges onto a wire rack and peel off the baking paper. Leave to cool.

3 Mix together the sponge ingredients for the smaller, top-tier cakes, as before, and bake for 15–20 minutes, until a skewer inserted into the centres comes out clean. Turn out onto a wire rack and leave to cool.

4 Meanwhile, make the lemon curd. Whisk together the cornflour and 100ml of water to a smooth paste. Place in a small pan and stir in the sugar and lemon juice.

5 Cook on a medium heat, stirring occasionally, until all the sugar has dissolved, then keep stirring until the mixture has thickened and you can no longer taste the cornflour.

6 Turn the heat down to low and add the soya milk and coconut oil. Stir briskly until the oil has melted and the mixture is smooth, then pour into the shallow metal tray, cover with cling film and freeze for about 45 minutes.

7 Make the biscuits. Add all the dry ingredients and vanilla to a bowl, then rub in the coconut oil. Add 20–25ml of water and combine to a dough ball.

8 Roll out the dough on a floured worktop to about 6mm thick. Cut out three mushroom shapes and three fox shapes.

Continues overleaf

Vegan Lavender & Lemon Fox Cake *continued*

FOR THE ROYAL ICING
100ml aquafaba
500g icing sugar, sifted
orange food-colouring
    paste or gel
honey-gold food-colouring
    paste or gel
brown food-colouring
    paste or gel
½ tsp cocoa powder

FOR THE VEGAN BUTTERCREAM
175g block of vegetarian
    spread, diced
375g vegetable shortening
500g icing sugar, sifted
pink food-colouring
    paste or gel
dark green food-colouring
    paste or gel
light green food-colouring
    paste or gel
lime green food-colouring
    paste or gel

YOU WILL NEED
23cm round, deep cake tins x 3,
    greased, then base-lined
    with baking paper
18cm round, deep cake tins x 3,
    greased, then base-lined
    with baking paper
shallow metal tray
baking tray lined with
    baking paper
6 small disposable piping bags
large disposable piping bag
26cm round, thin cake board
20cm round, thin cake board
cake-decorating turntable
tall side scraper
4 dowels
cocktail stick
large piping bag fitted with
    a medium closed star nozzle
large piping bag fitted with
    a small petal nozzle

Place on the lined baking tray and bake for about 8–10 minutes, until slightly browned at the edges. Transfer to a wire rack to cool.

9 Meanwhile, make the royal icing. Beat 75ml of the aquafaba in a stand mixer fitted with the beater, on medium–high speed until frothy, then add half the icing sugar and mix on a medium–low speed until smooth.

10 Add the remaining icing sugar and mix until the icing leaves a ribbon trail when you lift the beater. Add more icing sugar if the mixture is too runny.

11 Spoon about two thirds of the royal icing into a medium bowl, then divide this into three unequal portions – you'll need slightly more of one portion than the other two.

12 Colour the larger portion with orange colouring and a tiny amount of the honey-gold to make orange with a tinge of golden brown. Add the brown colouring and cocoa powder to one of the smaller portions for a deep brown colour. Leave the remaining portion white.

13 Divide the icing colours into the small piping bags as follows, and set aside:
» Orange: ¼ into 1 piping bag and ¾ into another.
» Brown: all into 1 piping bag.
» White: ¼ into 1 piping bag and ¾ into another.

14 Add enough orange colouring to give a bright orange colour to the remaining icing in the mixer bowl, and stir in 1 tablespoon of aquafaba at a time, until the icing is runny enough for a controlled 'drip' on the side of a cake tin. Cover with cling film and set aside.

15 Make the buttercream. Put the spread into the clean bowl of a stand mixer fitted with the beater and mix on a low–medium speed until smooth. Mix in the vegetable shortening until smooth and combined.

16 Mix in one third of the icing sugar until combined, then add the remaining icing sugar, gradually increasing the speed each time, until the buttercream is white and smooth. Put half the buttercream into the large disposable piping bag. Divide and colour the remainder as follows, and set aside:

» About 150g buttercream coloured pink.
» About 150g buttercream coloured dark green.
» About 2 tablespoons of buttercream coloured light green. Leave the remainder in the bowl.

17 Assemble the base. Place the larger cake board on the icing turntable. Snip a large tip on the piping bag of white buttercream and pipe a blob on the cake board. Top with a large sponge.

18 Spread a little buttercream from the bowl over the surface of the cake and, from the piping bag, pipe a white buttercream 'dam' around the top edge of the cake (this is to stop the lemon curd seeping out). Spoon 2–3 tablespoons of the lemon curd on top and spread evenly. Repeat with a second large sponge and then top with the third large sponge.

19 Spread the white buttercream from the bowl on top of the cake and around the sides. Spread a few smears of pink buttercream here and there on the sides. Smooth the top, then smooth the sides using the icing scraper. Aim for a thin crumb coat. Insert dowels into the cake and transfer to the fridge.

20 Assemble the top tier. Place the smaller cake board onto the turntable and stack and ice the smaller sponge layers just as you did for the base tier, except this time using dark green icing on the top and a combination of white and dark green buttercream on the sides.

21 Mark the outline of a fox shape on the top of the uppermost cake using the cocktail stick.

22 Snip a very small hole in the piping bag containing the smaller amount of orange royal icing, and snip a small–medium tip on the bag containing the larger amount of orange royal icing. Repeat for the white royal icing. Snip a small tip on the brown royal icing.

23 Use the small-tipped piping bags of orange and white royal icing to pipe the outline of the fox. Use the larger tipped bags to 'flood' the orange and white areas. Working quickly, use the cocktail stick to blend the white and orange by the tip of the

Continues overleaf

tail. Leave to set, then add the legs, nose and mouth.

24 Meanwhile, start piping the biscuits, piping the foxes in exactly the way you did for the cake. Pipe orange over the mushroom biscuits (outline first, then flooding), and pipe on white dots while the orange icing is still wet.

25 Remove the first cake tier from the fridge and place the second tier on top. Using a large spoon, pour the thinned orange icing in carefully controlled drips down the side of the bottom cake tier.

26 To make the roses and swirls, marble the pink buttercream with a little of the remaining white buttercream, but don't over mix, then divide it in half and place each half in a large piping bag – one fitted with the closed star nozzle and the other with the petal nozzle. Pipe swirls around the base of each tier and pipe roses on top.

27 Colour any remaining white buttercream with lime green, place this in the remaining small piping bag. Snip the end into a V shape and pipe tiny green leaves between the roses.

28 Decorate the cake with the fox and mushroom biscuits.

Aquafaba creates a less stable meringue than egg white, so it's best to make the layers for this stack in advance, then assemble just before serving.

Strawberries & 'Cream' Vegan Meringue Cake

400ml aquafaba
1 tsp cream of tartar
540g caster sugar
seeds of 1 vanilla pod
2 tsp xanthan gum
100g vegan white chocolate
 drops, melted

FOR THE COCONUT CREAM
3 x 400ml cans of good-quality
 coconut milk, refrigerated
 overnight
2 tsp vanilla paste

TO DECORATE
650g, strawberries, hulled
 and sliced (reserve a few
 whole and halved fruits
 for decoration)

YOU WILL NEED
4 baking sheets, greased,
 then lined with baking paper
large piping bag fitted with
 a large closed star nozzle
large cake-decorating
 paintbrush

1 Heat the oven to 120°C/100°C fan/235°F/Gas ¾. Draw a 20cm circle on each sheet of baking paper lining the trays, and turn the paper upside down so that the marking is on the underside.

2 To make the meringue, pour the aquafaba into a stand mixer fitted with the whisk. Add the cream of tartar and whisk on medium speed for 3–5 minutes, until foaming. Increase the speed to high and whisk for 5–10 minutes to stiff peaks.

3 Add the sugar, 1 tablespoon at a time, whisking between each addition to a stiff meringue. Add the vanilla seeds and sift the xanthan gum over the meringue. Whisk for a further 30 seconds.

4 Spoon the mixture into the large piping bag fitted with a star nozzle and pipe four discs of meringue with a decorative edge, using the circles you've drawn on the paper as guides, onto the baking sheets.

5 Bake the meringue discs for 2½ hours, until crisp and firm (they may still feel a little soft underneath). Remove from the oven and leave on the trays to cool.

6 Carefully turn over each disc and peel off the baking paper, leaving the meringues' undersides upwards.

7 Melt the chocolate in a bowl set over a pan of gently simmering water, then gently paint the chocolate over the base of each meringue and allow the chocolate to set.

8 To make the coconut cream, spoon out the layer of solid coconut milk at the top of each chilled can into a bowl (taking care not to add any of the watery liquid at this stage). Add the vanilla and whisk with an electric hand whisk until smooth, adding 1–2 tablespoons of the coconut water to loosen, if necessary.

Continues overleaf

9 To assemble the cake, place the first disc on a cake plate. Neatly spread one quarter of the coconut cream over the meringue, all the way to the edge. Place strawberry slices around the edge in a neat ring. Fill the middle of the ring with a layer of strawberries to cover the cream, using about one third of the strawberries altogether.

10 Place another meringue disc on top and repeat the process of spreading cream and placing strawberry slices as in Step 9. Repeat for another layer, then top with the last meringue disc. Spread over the remaining coconut cream and decorate the top of the cake with the reserved whole and halved strawberries. Serve immediately.

This is a quick-to-make and very pretty crowd-pleaser of a traybake – serve it with ice-cream for an after-supper treat, or enjoy it just as it is.

Gluten-free Cherry & Pistachio Traybake

340g unsalted butter, softened
270g golden caster sugar
6 eggs
185g gluten-free self-raising flour, sifted
2 tsp gluten-free baking powder
225g ground pistachio
200g cherries, halved and pitted

YOU WILL NEED
34 x 23cm roasting tin, greased, then lined (base and sides) with baking paper

1 Heat the oven to 200°C/180°C fan/400°F/Gas 6.

2 Beat the butter and sugar in a stand mixer fitted with the beater, on medium speed for 1–2 minutes, until pale and creamy.

3 With the mixer on a low speed, add the eggs, one at a time, beating well between each addition.

4 In a separate bowl, mix the self-raising flour, baking powder and ground pistachio together.

5 Using a metal spoon, fold the dry mixture into the wet mixture until incorporated.

6 Carefully fold the cherries into the mixture until evenly distributed, then pour the batter into the prepared tin.

7 Bake the sponge for 25–30 minutes, until golden brown and a skewer inserted into the centre comes out clean. Leave to cool completely in the tray, then cut into 16 equal pieces.

We have chosen raspberries and raspberry jam for the topping and filling of this vegan version of the much-loved Victoria sponge, but rustic blackberry or classic strawberry are also delicious.

Vegan Victoria Sponge

FOR THE SPONGE
300ml soya milk
1 tbsp apple cider vinegar
    or lemon juice
220g golden caster sugar
175g dairy-free spread
2 tsp vanilla paste
325g self-raising flour, sifted
1 tsp baking powder

**FOR THE FILLING
& DECORATION**
75g dairy-free spread
150g icing sugar,
    plus extra for dusting
1 tbsp vanilla paste
2 tbsp soya milk
150g homemade or good-
    quality raspberry jam
a handful of raspberries,
    to decorate

YOU WILL NEED
20cm sandwich tins x 2,
    greased, then lined
    (base and sides)
    with baking paper

1 Heat oven to 200°C/180°C fan/400°F/Gas 6.

2 Put the soya milk in a jug and add the vinegar. Leave for 5 minutes, to curdle slightly.

3 Beat the sugar, spread and vanilla in a stand mixer fitted with the beater, on medium–high speed for 5 minutes, until pale and creamy.

4 With the mixer on a low speed, gradually add the curdled soya milk, beating for 1 minute, until combined. Add the flour and baking powder, and mix on low until just incorporated.

5 Divide the cake mixture equally between the prepared tins and bake for 25–30 minutes, until a skewer inserted into the centres comes out clean. Allow the cakes to cool in the tins for 5 minutes, then turn out onto a wire rack to cool completely.

6 While the cakes are cooling, make the filling. Put the spread, icing sugar and vanilla in the bowl of a stand mixer fitted with the beater and beat on a low speed for 2–3 minutes, until fluffy. Beat in the soya milk, a little at a time, to loosen the mixture (you may not need all the soya milk).

7 To assemble, place one of the cooled sponges top-side downwards on a cake plate. Spread the jam over the cake, then spoon the filling over the jam, spreading it evenly to the edges.

8 Place the second cake, top-side upwards, on top of the filling. Dust with icing sugar, then top with raspberries, to decorate.

CONVERSION TABLES

WEIGHT

METRIC	IMPERIAL	METRIC	IMPERIAL	METRIC	IMPERIAL	METRIC	IMPERIAL
25g	1oz	200g	7oz	425g	15oz	800g	1lb 12oz
50g	2oz	225g	8oz	450g	1lb	850g	1lb 14oz
75g	2½oz	250g	9oz	500g	1lb 2oz	900g	2lb
85g	3oz	280g	10oz	550g	1lb 4oz	950g	2lb 2oz
100g	4oz	300g	11oz	600g	1lb 5oz	1kg	2lb 4oz
125g	4½oz	350g	12oz	650g	1lb 7oz		
140g	5oz	375g	13oz	700g	1lb 9oz		
175g	6oz	400g	14oz	750g	1lb 10oz		

VOLUME

METRIC	IMPERIAL	METRIC	IMPERIAL	METRIC	IMPERIAL	METRIC	IMPERIAL
30ml	1fl oz	150ml	¼ pint	300ml	½ pint	500ml	18fl oz
50ml	2fl oz	175ml	6fl oz	350ml	12fl oz	600ml	1 pint
75ml	2½fl oz	200ml	7fl oz	400ml	14fl oz	700ml	1¼ pints
100ml	3½fl oz	225ml	8fl oz	425ml	¾ pint	850ml	1½ pints
125ml	4fl oz	250ml	9fl oz	450ml	16fl oz	1 litre	1¾ pints

US CUP

INGREDIENTS	1 CUP	¾ CUP	⅔ CUP	½ CUP	⅓ CUP	¼ CUP	2 TBSP
Brown sugar	180g	135g	120g	90g	60g	45g	23g
Butter	240g	180g	160g	120g	80g	60g	30g
Cornflour (corn starch)	120g	90g	80g	60g	40g	30g	15g
Flour	120g	90g	80g	60g	40g	30g	15g
Icing sugar (powdered/confectioner)	100g	75g	70g	50g	35g	25g	13g
Nuts (chopped)	150g	110g	100g	75g	50g	40g	20g
Nuts (ground)	120g	90g	80g	60g	40g	30g	15g
Oats	90g	65g	60g	45g	30g	22g	11g
Raspberries	120g	90g	80g	60g	40g	30g	--
Salt	300g	230g	200g	150g	100g	75g	40g
Sugar (granulated)	200g	150g	130g	100g	65g	50g	25g
Sugar (caster/superfine)	225g	170g	150g	115g	75g	55g	30g
Sultanas/raisins	200g	150g	130g	100g	65g	50g	22g
Water/milk	250ml	180ml	150ml	120ml	75ml	60ml	30ml

LINEAR

METRIC	IMPERIAL		METRIC	IMPERIAL		METRIC	IMPERIAL		METRIC	IMPERIAL
2.5cm	1 in		7.5cm	3 in		13cm	5 in		20cm	8 in
3cm	1¼ in		8cm	3¼ in		14cm	5½ in		21cm	8¼ in
4cm	1½ in		9cm	3½ in		15cm	6 in		22cm	8½ in
5cm	2 in		9.5cm	3¾ in		16cm	6¼ in		23cm	9 in
5.5cm	2¼ in		10cm	4 in		17cm	6½ in		24cm	9½ in
6cm	2½ in		11cm	4¼ in		18cm	7 in		25cm	10 in
7cm	2¾ in		12cm	4½ in		19cm	7½ in			

SPOON MEASURES

METRIC	IMPERIAL
5ml	1 tsp
10ml	2 tsp
15ml	1 tbsp
30ml	2 tbsp
45ml	3 tbsp
60ml	4 tbsp
75ml	5 tbsp

COOK'S NOTES

Oven temperatures: Ovens vary – not only from brand to brand, but from the front to the back of the oven, as well as (in a non-fan oven) between the top and bottom shelves. Get to know your oven, and where its hotspots are, and invest in a cooking thermometer if you can. Always preheat the oven, and use dry oven gloves.

Eggs: Eggs should be at room temperature for baking cakes, unless specified. Some recipes may contain raw or partially cooked eggs. Pregnant women, the elderly, babies and toddlers, and people who are unwell should be aware of these recipes.

Herbs and fruit: Use fresh herbs and fresh, medium-sized fruit unless the recipe specifies otherwise.

Salt: If a recipe calls for a small, or hard-to-weigh amount, a ½ teaspoon fine salt weighs 2.5g, and a ¼ teaspoon weighs 1.25g. If you're using sea salt it is best to crush the flakes into a fine powder before measuring and adding to your recipe (unless specified).

Spoon measures: All teaspoons and tablespoons are level unless otherwise stated.

INDEX

This book is published to accompany the television series entitled
The Great British Bake Off, broadcast on Channel 4 in 2019

The Great British Bake Off® is a registered trademark of
Love Productions Ltd

Series produced for Channel 4 Television by Love Productions

First published in Great Britain in 2019 by Sphere

10 9 8 7 6 5 4 3 2

The Great British Bake Off: The Big Book of Amazing Cakes

ISBN 9780751574661

A CIP catalogue record for this book is available from
the British Library.

Picture Credits
Every effort has been made to trace and acknowledge copyright
holders. Any errors or omissions are unintentional and we will,
if informed, make necessary corrections in future editions of this
book. **Garden Photo Library:** pp.65 bottom left (Derek St Romaine/
GardenPhotoLibrary); **Getty Images:** pp.249 (Geography Photos/
Universal Images Group), 271 (Tim Graham); and **Shutterstock:**
pp.4–5 (Alik Mulikov), 73–4 (Matt Gibson), 213 (Matthew J Thomas),
229 (Kirsty Matt).

New recipes developed and written by: Juliet Sear,
Becca Watson and Mitzie Wilson

Editorial Director: Hannah Boursnell
Project Editor: Judy Barratt
Design & Art Direction: Smith & Gilmour
Food Photography: Faith Mason (except pp.1, 10 bottom left,
12, 21 top left, 79 bottom left, 82, 110, 130, 190, 236, 239, 200, 262:
Jamie Orlando-Smith; and pp.16, 18, 39, 40, 94: Smith & Gilmour)
Set & Landscape Photography: Kate Whitaker
Baker Photography: Mark Bourdillon
Food Stylists: Lisa Harrison and Isla Murray
Assistant Food Stylists: Evie Harbury and India Whiley-Morton
Additional Food Styling: Lottie Covell, Helen Stewart and
Rebecca Woods
Props Stylist: Olivia Wardle
Editorial Consultant: Nicola Graimes
Editorial Assistant: Simon Osunsade
Production Manager: Abby Marshall
Cover Photography: Jamie Orlando-Smith
Cover Food Stylist: Rebecca Woods
Cover Design: Smith & Gilmour

Publisher's thanks also to: Eliza Barratt, Hilary Bird, Georgina Cope,
Ingrid Court-Jones, Emma Marsden and Andy and Tor Sanders

Typeset in Archer & Gill Sans
Colour origination by Born Group
Printed and bound in Italy by L.E.G.O. SpA

Papers used by Sphere are from well-managed forest and other
responsible sources.

Sphere
An imprint of Little, Brown Book Group,
Carmelite House, 50 Victoria Embankment,
London EC4Y 0DZ

An Hachette UK Company
www.hachette.co.uk
www.littlebrown.co.uk

WITH THANKS

Love Productions would like to thank the following people:
Producer: Chloë Avery
Challenge producer: Tallulah Radula-Scott
Food Team: Katy Bigley, Georgia Harding, Emma Hair
Home Economist: Becca Watson
Love Executives: Letty Kavanagh, Rupert Frisby, Kieran Smith, Anna Beattie
Publicists: Amanda Console and Shelagh Pymm
Commissioning Editors: Kelly Webb-Lamb, Sarah Lazenby

Thank you to Paul, Prue, Noel and Sandi. And to the bakers for their recipes: Alice, Amelia, Dan, David,
Helena, Henry, Jamie, Michael, Michelle, Phil, Priya, Rosie and Steph; Andrew, Beca, Briony, Edd, Flora,
Frances, Jo, John, Kim-Joy, Liam, Mary-Anne, Miranda, Nancy, Rahul, Rob, Selasi, Sophie and all the
GBBO bakers from the last ten years.